I0435175

Welcome

Expressions of Consciousness
2nd book of the *Bubbles of Consciousness* book series

Together ~ thru the challenges of today ~
~ and into the promises of tomorrow

to the

Bubbles

of

Consciousness

book

series

Expressions of Consciousness
2nd book of the *Bubbles of Consciousness* book series

Expressions

of

Consciousness

by
Joseph Heirling

Together ~ thru the challenges of today ~
~ and into the promises of tomorrow

2014 © Joseph Heirling
joseph@heirling.com

Expressions of Consciousness
2nd book of the *Bubbles of Consciousness* book series

We Are

"bubbles of consciousness"

Floating Together

Thru the challenges of Today

And

Into the Promises of Tomorrow

Together ~ thru the challenges of today ~
~ and into the promises of tomorrow

let's

get

started

Expressions of Consciousness
2nd book of the *Bubbles of Consciousness* book series

Greetings

Dear Reader,

Welcome to this second book in our series exploring our collective human consciousness. The aim of this *Bubbles of Consciousness* series of books is ~ as mentioned in our earlier book *The Edges of Consciousness* ~ to quickly affect a change in humanity's somewhat self-destructive behaviors ~ that is, those behaviors that are steadily and increasingly poisoning our planet, our environment, and ourselves.

You may recall that the guiding assumption in developing this series is that our values and thoughts determine our behavior, and that in turn, our behavior impacts our environment for better, or for worse. In this series, topics touched upon will include (1) human history, psychology, and sociology, (2) extra sensory perception, paranormal experience and parapsychology, and (3) spirituality, transcendentalism, mysticism, religion, and the supernatural.

In the first book, *Edges of Consciousness*, we explored (1) paranormal phenomena such as psychokinesis, telekinesis, telepathy, teleportation, clairvoyance, precognition, out of body experiences, ghosts, and reincarnation, (2) the possibility that there is far more to us than we consciously realize, and (3) that our hidden gifts may be helpful in pursuing our goal of saving our planet Earth from humanity's misguided adventures. This book did not attempt to persuade through argumentation, but rather through a comprehensive review of what is known today about paranormal phenomena, especially through the eyes of rigorous and objective scientific researchers.

Paranormal research is very much an ongoing activity, and there is much happening today that most of us are not aware of. This book brought us relatively up-to-date on current research activity, and the interesting possibilities that become evident from that research. Most of this is happening at the outer edges of our everyday normal, or conventional, mundane collective consciousness.

Over the ages, our transcendent abilities have been generally disparaged by conventional thinking. Consequently, these transcendent abilities are still mysterious to most of us, and are broadly dismissed as belonging to the realm of the mystical, the paranormal, or the occult. In our exploration, we discovered that we happen to possess five distinct and fascinating transcendent abilities. These five transcendent abilities may offer meaningful help to us as we struggle to cope with the alarming challenges facing us here on our planet Earth.

In this second book, *Expressions of Consciousness*, we explore conventional thinking around the globe. Conventional thinking "per se" is investigated by examining a sample of today's major conventional thinkings ~ in alphabetic order ~ Buddhism, Capitalism, Christianity, Communism, Confucianism, Daoism, Hinduism, Individualism, Islamism, Judaism, and Science.

We submit these selected samples to a common analytic grid, with an eye to our goal of quickly turning our planetary situation around. In our ordered evaluation of the samples, we only question to what degree the various conventional thinkings examined could contribute to our quest for a fast, relative utopia. No other valuation is assigned to any of the samples.

We explore, a bit more thoroughly, the nature of conventional thinking, including its genesis and its dynamic effect on inter-generational human thought, together with its importance to our purpose. We also note that, given the nature of conventional thinking, modifying it in any way can be an arduous undertaking ~ and that any successful attempt at modification will usually be characterized by a very determined original thinker hand-in-hand with some very good luck.

Subsequent books in the *Bubbles of Consciousness* book series will continue the exploration of collective human consciousness by examining related areas. The historical roots underpinning conventional thinking will be charted. Lesser-known alternatives to conventional thinking will also be looked at, and possibilities probed for usefulness.

In this *Bubbles of Consciousness* book series exploring collective human consciousness, the ultimate hope is that paths will be discovered and utilized in such a way so as to help us reclaim the beauty and well-being of our awesome planet Earth, and save ourselves in the process.

All of us enjoy life here on this planet, and presently humanity is at risk of losing that existence. The signs of imminent environmental collapse are all around us.

This book is dedicated to all those who are making the effort to quickly turn things around.

Again, kindly be gentle with any editing errors. One can proofread a document until the eyeballs glaze over, but at a certain point the manuscript must be turned over to its readers.

The enduring Love and constant support that I was privileged to receive from my beloved wife, Ramona, during the drafting of this *Bubbles of Consciousness* book series is the treasure of a lifetime.

Joseph Heirling

Together ~ thru the challenges of today ~
~ and into the promises of tomorrow

Table of Contents

Expressions of Consciousness
2nd book of the *Bubbles of Consciousness* book series

Chapter 1 – Set up ~ What We Propose to Do

In this book we are going to look at a sample of today's more popular conventional thinkings. We'll view these different types of conventional thinking as various "expressions" of collective human consciousness. However, before we put our list of samples together, we need to nail down some basics. For example, just what is "conventional thinking?" We need to give the term *conventional thinking* a working definition before we start examining our samples.

An interesting and perhaps useful way to conceptualize the term *conventional thinking* is to think of it as a sort of philosophy-of-life. Throughout this book we will often use the terms "expression of consciousness" and "conventional thinking" and "philosophy-of-life" interchangeably, since their definitions have a lot in common. In fact, we can think of a philosophy-of-life as a type of conventional thinking and vice versa, and in turn we can think of both of them as types of expressions of collective human consciousness, to the degree that they may structure ongoing collective human consciousness.

Philosophies-of-life lay out basic assumptions about human existence, and given those assumptions, dictate how a good, respectable life is to be lived. From the basic assumptions a sacred goal is determined; by "sacred" we mean a goal as important ~ or more important ~ than life itself. Following the prescribed route to the sacred goal would be living a good, respectable life according to the tenets of whatever philosophy-of-life is structuring an individual's consciousness. The goal is sacred because it is considered to be so important that, if necessary, one would sacrifice life itself in order to achieve the goal.

Another way of thinking about the sacredness of a goal is that sacredness implies that life would become meaningless and not worth living if the sacred goal was not pursued with all the energy that one can muster during one's lifetime. In a philosophy-of-life scenario, the basic assumptions are the starting point, the sacred goal is the finish line, and the proper "race" from the starting point to the finish line is "living a good, respectable life."

Where does conventional thinking come from? We'll devote an entire book in the *Bubbles of Consciousness* book series to that question. But, in the meantime, we can come up with a temporary working answer that will serve our immediate purpose as we examine our sample of "expressions" of conventional thinking.

Conventional thinking comes from the other human beings that nurture us in childhood, and are with us and surround us as we live our life. For the individual, conventional thinking comes from parents, teachers, employers, counselors, the mass media, etc. No one individual just thinks up conventional thinking all by itself. It is stuck into our brains by our early care givers and later by any others that we assign importance to in our lives. It can be thought of as culture, i.e., the conceptual legacy that one generation drills into the developing minds of the next generation. For any individual, that is where conventional thinking comes from.

The sheer power of cultural legacies is not to be taken lightly. It is quite dominant. Consider the following. Suppose we took two newly born identical twins, and transplanted them separately into two different cultures, or expressions of collective human consciousness. We could take them, let's say, from eastern Russia, and transplant one twin newborn into South America, and the other twin newborn into the island continent of Australia. If we reexamined them twenty-five years later, from their thought, speech, and behavior there would be absolutely no trace of their actual birth into eastern Russia, born to native Russians. One would be thoroughly South American, and the other would be thoroughly Australian. One would think and act like a South American, and the other would think and act like an Australian. Not only would there be no cultural trace within them of their original Russian birthplace and birth heritage, but these twins would have barely anything in common when it comes to ways of thinking, cultural values, and subsequent behaviors.

Such is the awesome power of cultural legacy ~ the way we are raised by our caretakers. Something to ponder on. We'll come back to this a little later.

There are many different variations of conventional thinking, or expressions of collective human consciousness, floating around out there. For manageability, we need to select just a handful for the purpose of immediate examination, but we also need to make sure that the ones we pick are somehow important to present-day humanity. So, we will be guided by how currently popular the particular philosophy-of-life is ~ or ~ how important it is to global humanity, whether historically or within the present-day milieu.

Following these guidelines for picking our sample of major expressions of human conventional thinking yields the following for examination, in alphabetical order:

Buddhism

Capitalism

Christianity

Communism

Confucianism

Daoism

Hinduism

Individualism

Islam

Judaism

Science

When we get thru examining this sampling of conventional thinking, we will have a much better idea of what conventional thinking is, some of the different variations out there, and the degree to which they can be helpful to our own goal of quickly revitalizing our planetary home so that it can continue to sustain human life as we would like to enjoy it.

So far, to recap, we have (1) arrived at a working understanding of the term *conventional thinking*, we have (2) established in an elementary way where it comes from, and we have (3) put together a sample set for examination. Now we need to set up an analytical grid to guide us through our examination. To keep our investigation on a level playing field, we need to make sure that we examine each sample in the same way. We will do that by subjecting each sample to the same common questions, determined by the interests and needs of our purpose.

First, we want to know exactly what are the basic assumptions of the conventional thinking under examination. Basic assumptions are very special, and quite important. Basic assumptions are the grounding "facts" within a way of thinking that are unquestioned, and taken on sheer faith ~ without independent proof required. They are the foundation upon which the superstructure of the philosophy-of-life is built, and the starting point for the race to the sacred goal. To the degree that the basic assumptions are valid, the foundation for the superstructure is solid. But, to the degree that the basic assumptions may be invalid, the entire philosophy-of-life is subject to collapse when the foundation melts away. It is the difference between building on shifting sand or building on solid rock. Since the basic assumptions support and underpin everything else within the philosophy-of-life, we want to know exactly what those assumptions are. That will get us very quickly to the essence of the conventional thinking that we are analyzing as we work our way thru the sample set.

Second, we want to know what the "sacred" goal is ~ a goal so sacred that life is viewed as a means of getting to the sacred goal; life is not viewed as an end in itself. A goal so sacred that lack of achievement would cause one's life to be viewed as a failure. A goal so sacred that everything else in life pales in comparison, with the sacredness of the goal demanding that every bit of one's energy and time during one's lifetime be devoted to the pursuit of the sacred goal. Those getting to the sacred goal are looked up to as winners and heroes, with the others viewed as losers and failures. We expect the sacred goal to be linked in some way to the basic, starting assumptions set forth by the conventional thinking that we are analyzing. Does the sacred goal make sense given the grounding assumptions laid down?

Third, once we have established the starting assumptions and the sacred goal for the conventional thinking we are looking at, we want to know what route is prescribed to get to the sacred goal. Are there any sacred texts to be followed? Any prophets or holy figures or wizards or founding thinkers to be acknowledged and listened to? Any special days of the calendar to be observed? Any rituals to be followed? Exactly what steps are proposed by the philosophy-of-life that will lead an individual to attainment of the sacred goal? What are the consequences of failure? Is the goal actually attainable in the same lifetime that it is being pursued? Are certain sacrifices required, and if so, what are those sacrifices?

Fourth, how does the conventional thinking want the individual to view itself? Or, what is the definition of self that is offered to the individual by the philosophy-of-life? If the individual asked ~ What am I? ~ how would the conventional thinking answer? According to the philosophy-of-life, what is the individual's place in human reality? Is it good? Is it evil? Is it innocent? Is it damned? Is it something? Is it nothing? Exactly how is it defined by the conventional thinking structuring the individual's consciousness? How is the individual to consider itself? How is it to treat itself?

Fifth, ditto for the "other." How does the conventional thinking want the individual to view others? Or, what is the definition of other offered to the individual by the philosophy of life? If the individual asked ~ What are these other human beings? ~ how would the conventional thinking answer? According to the philosophy-of-life, what are the others' place in human reality? Is it good? Is it evil? Is it innocent? Is it damned? Is it something? Is it nothing? Exactly how is it defined by the conventional thinking structuring the individual's consciousness? How is the individual to consider others like itself? How is it to treat others?

Sixth, what is the nature of the boundary between self and other set forth by the philosophy-of-life? Is there a boundary? Maybe there isn't. But if there is some sort of boundary separating self and others, what is it? Can it be breached? Can self ever become like other? Can other ever become like self? What does the philosophy-of-life say about the relationship between self and other?

Expressions of Consciousness
2nd book of the *Bubbles of Consciousness* book series

Seventh, given our driving desire to quickly turn things around on our planet, and achieve some sort of utopia compared to the issues and problems that we are experiencing now, we are most interested in what the philosophy-of-life, or conventional thinking, has to say about utopias here and now. Does it acknowledge the concept of a utopia? If it does, when does it consider it attainable? How is utopia achieved? What is its nature? Given the philosophy-of-life's assumptions, sacred goals, prescribed routes, and dictated stances toward self and toward other ~ is the nature of its utopia attainable and desirable?

These seven questions will form our analytical grid, and we will subject each of our samples to these seven questions:

- ◆ basic, starting assumptions
- ◆ sacred goal
- ◆ prescribed route to sacred goal
- ◆ stance toward self
- ◆ stance toward other
- ◆ nature of boundary between self and other
- ◆ stance toward utopia on earth

In that way we will determine, for each sample, the possible answers to these questions. The playing field will be level because we will look at each sample through the lens of the same seven questions. Hopefully, we will be able to determine to what degree each examined sample may be helpful to our overriding goal ~ remember ~ quickly turning around a rapidly deteriorating situation here on our planet and bringing about a utopia relative to what we are struggling with right now.

Chapter 2 – Caveats ~ What We Propose Not to Do

Now that we have established an analytical grid to assist us in our examination of our sample set of conventional think-ings, we need to limit that examination so that it is evenhanded and fair to the samples. We want to make sure that we do not wander in our examination, but stay focused to our purpose. It is ever so easy for one's mind to wander when dealing with philosophies-of-life. They are so very fascinating because they speak to our deeper natures and needs and desires. We want to make sure that mind-wandering doesn't happen while we review each sample. So, let's set up some stop signs, so to speak.

We are going to examine each sample individually, and not compare it to other samples. Even though elements of more than one philosophy-of-life commingle in varying de-grees within all individuals, the different belief systems have to be analyzed separately in order to distinguish their distinctive essences. In examining the samples, we are not interested in "valuing" the samples, but only in understanding what each one has to say and offer to the individual. If at times we do feel the need to "compare" samples, it will have to be within the purview of the seven examination questions. If after examination we feel the need to put "values" on the samples, it will have to be strictly within the purview of the seventh examination question alone ~ stance toward utopia on earth. After all, that is the purpose of this *Bubbles of Consciousness* series of books on our collective human consciousness.

The eleven philosophies-of-life that we have selected for examination have many variations of belief within them. Since we don't want to examine all the endless variations, but only a general overview, we will limit ourselves to looking only at the basic, general understandings within a particular conventional thinking. For example, within the conventional thought "communism" there may be variations in assumptions, beliefs, practices and goals. We will look only at the assumptions, beliefs, practices and goals common to all who subscribe to "communism" as their basic philosophy-of-life. That will help us keep the examination of our samples tight and efficient.

We will not look at the historical development of conventional thinking. That will be the purpose of our next book. Our approach in this book is more present oriented. It answers the following questions. If we were born today into a particular culture, what would we be taught by our care givers? What would we be taught to accept as "truth" without question? What would we be taught is the sacred goal in life? What would we be taught are the proper means to achieve that sacred goal? What would we be taught about the individual? What would we be taught about others? What would we be taught about the relationship between the individual and others? Would we be taught the concept of "utopia?" And if so, what would we be taught about utopia? By keeping the examination along those lines, we will have the vicarious pleasure of finding out for ourselves how we would have turned out if we had been born into these different cultures, or philosophies-of-life, or conventional thinkings, all being differing expressions of collective human consciousness.

We will not be critical in our examination. Our intent is not to look at faults, imperfections, or inconsistencies. We do not intend to either discredit or promote any sample. Rather, our examination will be expository in nature. We simply seek to understand these philosophies-of-life, and how a life would be lived if we were born into a culture that was dominated by a particular conventional thought. Again, what does the philosophy-of-life say to the individual, and how is a life to be lived according to the prescribed guidelines? We are simply looking for uncomplicated, generalized answers for today's expressions of the conventional thinkings that we have selected for our sample.

A last caveat. We humans are curious creatures, and we always love to know what the other person is really, truly thinking. Earlier, we noted that the voices of more than one philosophy-of-life commingle in varying degrees within all individuals. It is the nature of the human experience. We are very social, and today most of us are increasingly sharing a global consciousness. To discern what philosophy-of-life or belief system is truly dominant in an individual's thinking, don't just observe the individual's practice or observance of calendar-driven rituals, but rather, also observe what philosophy-of-life or belief system they seem to adhere to when making stressful decisions in ordinary life. That is the best way to determine what is really driving an individual's thinking and behavior.

Let's start examining our samples, shall we?

Chapter 3 – Buddhism

Buddhism is a major human philosophy-of-life ~ or conventional thinking ~ or expression of collective human consciousness ~ followed by roughly 400 million to one billion people. Even though Buddhism is primarily identified with the Southeast Asian landmasses, Buddhist adherents can be found globally. Its ethical directives of moderation and compassion are universally attractive to a struggling humanity.

Primarily a mental, or meditative, pursuit, Buddhist practice is dominated by the historical figure born in ancient India as Siddhartha Gautama (variously spelled), who is revered by Buddhist followers as *the* Buddha. The practice of Buddhism is essentially conducted by following the teachings of this single founder, and since the teachings are somewhat metaphysically complex, we can expect to find ourselves spending a bit of time going over them. As we will shortly see, Gautama may have brought several original conceptualizations to human thinking. Close to one billion humans are trying their best to measure up to what Gautama declared is the ultimate truth and sacred goal in human life.

In his pursuit of the ultimate truth of human existence, a rather popular undertaking in the Hindu culture that he was born into, Gautama claimed to have discovered three fundamental truths about human existence. These claims cannot be either proven or disproved. One is either taught to believe in them, or not taught to believe in them. One either chooses to accept these Gautama teachings as fundamental truth, or one chooses to reject them. We call these Gautama teachings the foundational assumptions in Buddhism. Since they are the keystones of Buddhist thought, we'll examine these claimed discoveries one at a time.

In propounding these three alleged discoveries, Gautama accepted the prevailing Hindu concepts of karma and rebirth, but explained them in a rather unique "Buddhist" way. Gautama, too, assumes that the human experience is essentially an engagement, arranged and propelled by karma, into an unending cycle of rebirth. However, it is Gautama's unique explanation of the underlying causes and nature of karma and rebirth that fundamentally distinguishes Buddhism from the Hindi culture that he was born into.

Grounding Assumptions

Gautama claimed that his first discovery of the true nature of human existence was his personal determination that everything that we are conscious of is, in fact, without the reality, or substance, that we assume things to have. This first discovery is based on his observations that all phenomena are impermanent and constantly undergoing change. Impermanence, Gautama claims, is one of the basics of human existence. A popular Buddhist example is that of the flower blossom. First a bud, then a beautiful flower, then wilt and then rot. The beautiful flower is here now, then quickly gone. He argued that the flower cannot be something "in and of itself" because it is too fleeting, too impermanent.

Another example may help us catch Gautama's thought at a more subtle level.

Think of an ocean wave. The big ones are surfed all the time by our young people the world over. These young people really get into their surfing, personalizing the gigantic waves, and referring to them as if they have substance and an individuality of themselves, and perhaps even an agenda of their own too. But, think of it a little further. That big awesome ocean wave is not a thing in and of itself, but rather a confluence of ocean bottoms, sea currents, and atmospheric winds. That ocean wave is merely a "form" made out of sea water influenced by ocean bottoms and prevailing winds, conjured up for a fleeting moment by these processes, themselves also changing and impermanent. The ocean wave is not a thing in and of itself, but merely a form, or shape, of sea water temporarily materialized for a fleeting moment by constantly changing processes.

Gautama would argue that everything that we are conscious of is of the same nature ~ temporary illusionary forms conjured up for fleeting moments by processes fleeting and temporary and illusionary themselves.

Gautama's second claimed discovery is a very aggressive application of his first claimed discovery. When Gautama claimed that everything that we are conscious of is without any real inherent substance or reality, he really meant it. That illusionary impermanence includes our "selves." We say "I" and "me" and "mine," and most of us think that we are something real and substantial and permanent that pre-exists birth and survives death. We call it our "self" or "soul," as if we are something lasting and of true individual substance. Gautama says "not so." According to Gautama, even the concept of a personal self is false. Any "self" or "soul" that we may assume or conceptualize is unsubstantial, a fleeting and temporary illusion that is just as impermanent and fleeting as everything else that we are conscious of.

According to Gautama, one's "self" or "soul" is a fleeting thing, like the ocean wave, brought about for a moment in time by processes that are equally fleeting and temporary and impermanent.

Gautama's third claimed discovery is a conclusory application of his first two claimed discoveries. Gautama claims that human existence is essentially painful and laden with endless suffering.

Why? He says that we falsely think that we and all that we are conscious of are actually real things with individual substances. Gautama says that kind of thinking is delusional, which in turn brings about ill-advised clinging and unsatiated wanting, thereby engendering karma, resulting in endless rebirths pursuing ill-advised wants that can never be satisfied by fleeting, immaterial, impermanent things.

Based on these three "discoveries," Gautama formulated his four formal assumptions of human existence, which he taught to those around him. These four formal assumptions, in Buddhism, are called the *Four Noble Truths*, and are expected to be accepted without question.

The first of Gautama's *Four Noble Truths* says that human life is unending pain and suffering, and that the only certainties of human existence are sickness, aging, and death.

The second of Gautama's *Four Noble Truths* says that human suffering is caused by delusional thinking, which in turn engenders ill-advised clinging, which in turn engenders unsatiated wanting, which in turn triggers karma, which in turn energizes the endless wheel of rebirth.

The third of Gautama's *Four Noble Truths* says that suffering ends when delusional thinking ends, thereby destroying ill-advised clinging, which destroys unsatiated wanting, which in turn neutralizes karma, which then stops energizing the endless wheel of rebirth.

The fourth of Gautama's *Four Noble Truths* says that escape from this cycle of endless suffering is to be attained by following the path laid down by Gautama, primarily known in Buddhism as the *Noble Eightfold Path*.

Sacred Goal

In essence, thru his three alleged discoveries and subsequent formulation of his *Four Noble Truths*, Gautama is saying that there is really nothing for a human to live for. The goal in human life is to permanently escape from earthly, human existence just as quickly as one can. These are the unquestioned assumptions in Buddhism. If one accepts Gautama's *Four Noble Truths* without question, one can be a Buddhist. If one questions them, then, of course, one cannot, in good faith, be a Buddhist.

Gautama's sacred, and actually only, goal in life is to permanently escape from an endless cycle of rebirth characterized as unremitting pain and suffering. Attaining this release, or escape, is termed *nirvana*. Gautama says that the goal in life is to (1) get rid of the delusion of an individual ego, (2) thereby neutralizing clinging and wanting, (3) thereby avoiding any future rebirths. Freedom from the mechanics of karma and the endlessly turning wheel of rebirth, or reincarnation, is to be in a state of nirvana, or freedom ~ what Gautama says is the sacred goal in a human life.

Karma

Before we explore Gautama's recommended path to the freedom of nirvana, we had better take a closer look at this thing called *karma*. After all, karma is fingered as the mechanism that keeps the cycle of rebirth going. Buddhism offers a rather detailed explanation of how karma works, commonly known in Buddhist circles as "dependent origination." The Buddhist explanation presumes the cycle of rebirth, and concentrates on explaining how karma connects one expiring human life to another new human life, thereby keeping the wheel of rebirth endlessly turning.

According to the Buddhist explanation, a human dies in a general state of ignorance, delusion ~ and most importantly ~ with unfinished business ~ that is, unsatisfied wants and desires. This is karma per se, the unfinished business. These unsatisfied cravings act as karmic seeds to generate new human life. The karmic seeds engender new consciousness, which of course requires a body and a mind to act as a vehicle for the new consciousness. Once this new consciousness is housed in a mind and body, through contact with its surroundings it quickens with sensation and starts seeking to satisfy the unsatisfied cravings, or karmic seeds, that brought it into existence in the first place. Another birth and life are lived, again dying in ignorance, delusion, and with more unfinished business. That death leaves more karmic seeds behind, thereby keeping the wheel of rebirth spinning endlessly. This process is thought of as "dependent origination" because a rebirth is dependent upon a prior death leaving behind the karmic seeds of unsatisfied desires.

Gautama offers to free humanity from this assumed cycle of rebirth, because he has concluded, during his meditations, that human life is only endless pain and suffering, with the only certainties being sickness, aging, and death.

How does Gautama propose to guide humanity to his version of nirvana ~ escape from human existence and life? When he died, Gautama left three things behind: (1) his own life as an example, (2) his teachings, and (3) a community of Buddhist believers. In Buddhist circles, these three legacies are considered the *Three Jewels* of Buddhism.

Gautama's life has been extensively written about, so we won't concentrate on it here; we'll save that for our next book. However, in brief, Gautama was bought up in a very sheltered life of perfect health and wealth and youth. In young adulthood, when exploring the world outside of his very protected haven, he ran across instances of things less than ideal and perfect, e.g., disease, old age, and death. He was so startled by these new experiences that he decided to figure out for himself what was really going on, and what was real, and what wasn't real. Years of starving ascetic renunciation almost killed him, but didn't bring him the answers he wanted. So, giving up on ascetic renunciation, he sat under a tree and sunk into a deep meditation. When he came out of that deep meditation, he announced his three discoveries and the *Four Noble Truths*.

In Buddhism, his life of renunciation and meditation is considered the best example of how to live a human life, and because of that, his exemplary life is considered the first of the *Three Jewels* of Buddhism.

Path to the Sacred Goal

The second of the *Three Jewels* of Buddhism are Gautama's teachings, codified into his *Noble Eightfold Path*. The eight distinct points of Gautama's teachings are themselves grouped into three collections addressing (1) wisdom ~ how a Buddhist mind should be thinking, (2) morality ~ how a Buddhist mind should approach its world, and (3) mental discipline ~ what a Buddhist mind should be doing.

Under the rubric of Buddhist wisdom, we find two of the eight points of Gautama's *Noble Eightfold Path*. First, the Buddhist mind should apprehend human reality as it really is, not just as it appears to be. Second, the Buddhist mind, because of personal renunciation of the things of the world, should be characterized by a sense of personal freedom and harmlessness.

What about morality, or, how a Buddhist mind should approach its world? Under this rubric, the idea of harmlessness is further emphasized. First, one should not utter harmful words or speech. Second, one should not behave in a way harmful to other humans. And third, one's occupation should not harm oneself, others, or one's surroundings. The Buddhist mind should be so dominated by the concept of harmlessness that one's speech, behavior, and means of livelihood are above approach.

Under the rubric of mental discipline, we find the last three of the eight cardinal points of Gautama's *Noble Eightfold Path*. Thru (1) proper concentration, or meditation, the Buddhist mind should always (2) be trying to improve (3) how it perceives reality, because the increasing proper perception of reality will help eliminate improper craving, thereby minimizing the generation of karmic seeds ~ the essence of the sacred goal.

All told, between Gautama's *Four Noble Truths* and his *Noble Eightfold Path*, we have what is considered Gautama's *Middle Way* approach toward the goal of nirvana, or escape from human suffering. Harmlessness in all aspects of thought and behavior will generally lead to moderation in action. Correct meditation will keep one from becoming enamored by extreme philosophies, such as those philosophies espousing the disparate goals of either extreme poverty or extreme wealth. And, correct mental awareness will help one remember that things that are apparent are not really things in and of themselves. In focusing on Gautama's *Four Noble Truths* and his *Noble Eightfold Path* and his *Middle Way*, the Buddhist mind will find itself always acting in moderation, and will find itself always filled with compassion for others also caught in the grip of karma.

Buddhist Monks

The third of the *Three Jewels* of Buddhism is the Buddhist community ~ all those who, in some way, follow in Gautama's footsteps. Let's follow it closely here, because it is here that we will find the social practice of Buddhism, as opposed to the individual, meditative approach. The Buddhist community is divided into two groups, monks and laity. These two groups have a strong symbiotic relationship to each other. Let's start with the monks.

Buddhist monks are those who literally attempt to replicate the life of Gautama in their own lives. They renounce all worldly possessions, and plunge themselves into a meditative life seeking the enlightenments that Gautama claimed to have discovered in his own meditations. They attempt to live each and every one of the eight points of Gautama's *Noble Eightfold Path*, not only during their meditations, but also when they are not plunged into meditation. Their lives, as Buddhist monks, serve as living reminders to all those around them as to what Buddhism is all about. They lead the Buddhist community, using their own lives as spiritual examples, and provide guidance and counseling for dealing ~ in the Buddhist way ~ with the ordinary challenges of daily living. Of course, due to their vows of poverty, Buddhist monks need someone to take care of them during their extensive meditations, and that's where the Buddhist laity steps in.

While there are many who wish to live the life of a Buddhist monk, there are a much, much greater many who do not, even though they accept the Buddhist teachings. They may lack the will, or they may perhaps lack the mental discipline to relive Gautama's life. They may be in the family way ~ householders busy raising children with all the activity entailed by that. They may live in such a way that the long periods of quiet and repose necessary for prolonged meditation are not available to them. Yet, they do admire Gautama and his teachings, and they wish they could enter into his nirvana by following his *Noble Eightfold Path.*

Since they do not have the ability ~ due to whatever personal circumstance they may find themselves in ~ to relive his life as Buddhist monks attempt to do, they take the approach of proxy, and attempt to meet Gautama's sacred goal vicariously. They do this by taking diligent care of the Buddhist monks ~ assuming that by taking care of the monks some of the monks' goodness and karmic attainments will become theirs by proxy ~ in turn helping them vicariously minimize the generation of karmic seeds in their own lives.

Remember, according to Gautama, the elimination of karmic seeds is what it is all about. Pilgrimages to sacred sites, generous offerings to the monks, bowing, chanting, and celebrating sacred days in the Buddhist calendar are all part of the community practice of Buddhism in the pursuit of Gautama's sacred goal of permanently escaping from human existence.

Stance Toward Earthly Utopia

Let's recap a bit. We know that Buddhism's basic assumption is that human existence is painful, and we know that Buddhism's sacred goal is for everyone to escape from human existence as quickly as possible. We know that Buddhism's means to the goal is following the teachings of Gautama, especially, his *Noble Eightfold Path*. What about our other questions?

Given that Buddhism does not recognize the existence of an eternal soul, its stance toward the individual must be somewhat as follows. Whatever it is that is experiencing the suffering in a human life is probably defined along the lines of "a transient disturbed existence of an experiencing something within a causatively linked succession egotistically assuming itself to be an individual entity due to perceptual localization within the human existential situation." That's quite a mouthful, isn't it? Without the recognition of the existence of eternal souls, we are left with that rather mind-bending definition of the human individual. That "experiencing something" is urged, by Gautama, to practice harmlessness and moderation in all its actions in order to hasten escape from human existence and suffering.

Of course, given the same assumptions and arguments, Buddhism's stance toward other would be the same, i.e., "a transient disturbed existence of an experiencing something within a causatively linked succession egotistically assuming itself to be an individual entity due to perceptual localization within the human existential situation." Gautama's assertion is that everyone is experiencing the same impermanent things. That's why the Buddhist recommendation for compassion. Intelligent compassion helps one remember the reality underlying the appearances.

There is no real difference between self and other, unless it is the degree to which the individual and other differ in their progress toward the Buddhist sacred goal of permanently escaping human existence. Boundaries between self and other are only those imposed by discrete human bodies ~ vessels, so to speak, for individual consciousness. Outside of that, it is just countless karmic seeds endlessly sprouting into ever-new human lives.

In sum, despite its laudable position on human ethics and morality, Buddhism is not going to be a strong friend to anyone attempting to bring about a better state of affairs, or utopia, here on our planet Earth. Instead of wanting to change things for the better, Buddhism advocates escape, assuming that human existence will always be characterized by pain and suffering. Buddhism, because of its starting assumptions and final goal, does not necessarily appear to be a good philosophy-of-life for anyone wanting to improve humanity's lot on Earth right here and right now.

Chapter 4 – Capitalism

Since Capitalism is the most popular economic model in our world today, we need to take a close look at what it teaches to its followers. Practically everybody on our planet today is affected in some way by the capitalist creed ~ or instance of conventional thinking.

Why? How? Because to the degree that any individual uses modern products, those products are most likely produced by some type of capitalist industry located somewhere on our planet. Given that our collective thirst for modern products seems to be insatiable, and given that modern products can, at least today, be best produced by capitalist manufacturers, the expression of collective human consciousness that we term *Capitalism* does not currently face a competitive model that can mount a reasonable challenge in terms of economy of scale, technological innovation, and the mass production of consumer goods.

Some form of Capitalism is found everywhere, and consequently, Capitalism affects everyone, whether you are a believer or not. Simply being a capitalistic consumer supports the capitalistic way of life. One doesn't have to be a capitalist, per se. Just being a consumer of capitalistic produced goods keeps driving the capitalist system forward. So, just what is *Capitalism*?

Grounding Assumptions

Before we dive into the capitalist scriptures, so to speak, let's look at the grounding assumptions of Capitalism. It is a philosophy-of-life. Its sacred value is individual wealth, and consequently, its sacred goal is the maximization of individual wealth. Its grounding assumption is that the best way for an individual to define and value itself is by measuring how much material wealth, or capital, the individual possesses. The more individual wealth the individual possesses, the more the individual values itself. The less individual wealth the individual possesses, the less the individual values itself. It cuts both ways, and it is simple and direct. In Capitalism, individual wealth is both sacred and determining.

Did you notice how many times we used the word *individual* in the preceding paragraph? Lots of times, right? That leads us to the very essence of Capitalism, i.e., the concept of *privacy*. Capitalism does not espouse just the maximization of wealth, but the individual, or *private*, maximization of wealth. Capitalism wants *individuals* trying to become as wealthy as they can during their lifetimes. Without the concept of the private ownership of things, Capitalism cannot exist. Privacy, per se, is critically important to the human conventional thinking known as Capitalism. Let's explore a comparative example of this concept of individual ownership.

Some of the smaller cultures on our planet do not embrace the concept of individual ownership. Everything belongs to the group. In those cultures, if we were to leave our home, during our absence another member of the group could come in and freely take whatever was there, under the argument that we were not using it at the moment ~ and they needed it. We couldn't yell "theft," because everything belongs to the group, and not to any particular individual. The individual who has the most right at the moment to any particular item would be the individual with the most pressing need for it ~ at the moment, of course. The group owns everything; the individual owns nothing. Of course, in this kind of set-up, one cannot maximize individual wealth, because one cannot own anything as an individual. The group owns everything. "Individual wealth" is not a concept in these societies.

Capitalism is diametrically the opposite in terms of who owns what. Ownership of items belongs to individuals, not to the group. If someone enters into our home during our absence and takes something needed, we indeed quickly yell "theft," and the capitalist system will immediately send police to catch and punish the thief, no matter how pressing the thief's need was at the moment. If one person is idly sitting on a huge warehouse of unused chairs ~ and another individual enters that warehouse without permission and takes just one single chair to rest their weary body ~ the capitalist system will catch and punish that weary thief.

In a capitalist system, the concept of privacy and the right to own something privately is absolutely sacred, and any violation of private rights is severely penalized, even at times to the point of life and limb. That is why, in capitalist systems, there exists the grounding assumption that the most funda-mental duty of the group, or government, is to protect the right of individuals to privately own things. Under Capitalism, that's what much of law enforcement is all about, i.e., protect-ing individuals from thieves, trespassers, and other violators.

Sacred Goal

In sum, Capitalism teaches the sacredness of the right of the individual to possess, use, and own property to the exclu-sion of all other individuals. It teaches that the group's duty is to protect that sacred right of individual privacy and ownership. It suggests that because private ownership is paramount, an individual's self-worth and social-worth are best measured by an individual's wealth, or private holdings. And, because of that, it naturally follows that the sacred goal in life is to maximize private holdings, in order to maximize the measure of self-worth. These are the grounding assumptions upon which the edifice known as Capitalism is structured, and it teaches this as grounding concepts not to be questioned or challenged.

Types of Wealth

Wealth can be conceptualized in a variety of ways. For our purposes in understanding Capitalism as it is actually practiced in our world today, we wish to utilize a rather wide-ranging definition of wealth that will embrace all the popular capitalistic opportunities currently being exploited in today's wide-ranging capitalist expressions. For this purpose, we will think of one's "capital" or "wealth" as any asset that is exclusively possessed, used and owned by the individual ~ and that can be turned into profits, or money.

Let's list the possibilities, from the standpoint of a young person just stepping into responsible adulthood.

First, there are those commonly thought of things that are given to the young adult by its caretakers, usually in the form of gifts and inheritances. Second, there are the natural gifts and talents the young adult was born with. Third, there is the natural energy of the young adult that can be brought to bear on various enterprises. And fourth, there is the time of the young adult, which too can be harnessed in various ways ~ up to 24 hours each day.

All of these four forms of privately or personally owned capital, or wealth, can be turned into profits and money if handled correctly. The degree to which the young adult actually does that determines the degree to which it is viewed as truly responsible, at least thru the eyes of a capitalist culture. The correct mix and application of these four basic categories of personal wealth are necessary in order to enhance one's starting wealth with a stream of monetary profits, thereby augmenting and increasing personal wealth ~ the sacred goal, remember?

Of course, the assumption is that the group, or government, is busy protecting the right of the young adult to keep personal wealth private, including any gains made from that personal, or private, wealth.

To recap wealth-types before we move forward, in a capitalist culture where individual privacy and ownership are conceived as a sacred right, one's private wealth can be categorized in four distinctly different ways ~ (1) material possessions, (2) personal gifts and talents, (3) personal energy, and (4) personal time. These four types of wealth, in the appropriate mixes, can be utilized (i.e., invested) in a capitalistic fashion to generate even more individual wealth available for either further investment or static monetization. Now that we have that pinned down, let's review what passes as the capitalist scriptures. It will help us understand how Capitalism is practiced today.

Founding Documents

Not quite 300 years ago, a Scottish man by the name of Adam Smith (1723-1790) wrote a series of five books commonly known as *The Wealth of Nations*, published around 1776. If any manuscript can be considered the sacred scriptures of modern Capitalism, it would be Smith's. In each of his five books comprising *The Wealth of Nations*, Smith discusses extremely important aspects of modern Capitalism. These aspects are unusually important, because thru them Smith argues that if one desires to increase one's own wealth, one does not necessarily have to take it from another individual. Wealth can actually be "created" without harming another individual, perhaps even bettering the other individual in the process of capitalistic wealth "creation." Let's review these five extremely vital aspects of modern Capitalism one at a time.

In his first Book, Smith argues that the one single greatest generator of material wealth is the division, or specialization, of labor.

An example. Suppose that given a handful of kids in a large neighborhood, each wants to run a lemonade stand against all the others, the competition. Each one will have to set up the little stand, make the little pitcher of lemonade, set out the little cups, and then police the stand hoping that someone thirsty shows up. Each lemonade stand operator might make a few sales, if the day is lucky.

Now, the capitalist approach. The kids get together and come up with this novel idea ~ they will pool their resources, time, and talents. A couple of them will set up one big stand at the entrance to the neighborhood and man it during the day. Another will keep making lemonade, pitcher after pitcher. Another will keep cups in supply for thirsty customers. Another will post signs at the neighborhood entrance and greet people and cars coming by, and direct the traffic to the lemonade stand. Each kid gets really good at the particular assigned task.

The likelihood is that this division, or specialization, of labor will let the kids generate much more sales than if each had gone their separate way, especially given the fact that the kids, instead of competing against each other for thirsty customers, instead are now cooperating with each other in order to corral all the thirsty customers to their community stand.

Even after splitting the profits, each kid will realize much more profit than if it had run its own lemonade stand all by itself. That's the essence of Smith's argument. The division and specialization of labor create wealth, as if out of thin air, and without necessarily hurting anyone else. Production and sales volumes jump way, way up.

In his second Book, Smith discusses the need for capital ~ starting monies or stock ~ to be exact.

Let's stick with our lemonade stand. For the kids to pull off their plan, they will have to come up with resources before they make and sell that first pitcher of lemonade. They'll need lemonade mix, pitchers, cups, a table, chairs, directional signs, poster board materials, and other items. To get their hands on all that, they will have to come up with some starting money, whether begged, borrowed, or earned. That's what capital is ~ the starting resource that gets a business plan moving forward. Now, if some of the kids say that they don't have any money to put into the plan because they need it for something else, they can't join in. But, the kids who have some spare money that they don't need for personal needs can participate in the lemonade stand project, and share in the profits.

That's Smith's point. Division of labor by itself is not enough. One has to be able to set aside, or divert, money from personal needs to be able to fund the business plan. Monies invested in business plans is called capital, or stock. Obviously, any kid using all their personal earnings and/or allowances for personal needs such as going to movies and buying treats is not going to be able to participate in the lemonade project. They haven't set aside any money to join the project. However, the kids who can set aside and save will be able to help fund and join the project. Those kids have just become "capitalists," i.e., they had personal resources that they were able to provide as capital to the lemonade stand venture. They didn't spend those personal resources on personal needs.

In his third Book, Smith discusses the actual mechanics of the creation of value.

Again ~ the kids and their lemonade stand. First, they came up with their business plan. Then, they pooled their resources, or capital. What's next? Creation of value. How? It's very simple. Lemonade mix and water will be brought together to create the actual lemonade. Now the kids have a sellable product. That's what Smith is talking about in his third book. Value is created, as if out of thin air, by taking raw resources, mixing in some specialized labor, and producing finished products. One kid will mix the lemonade. Another will set up the table and chairs. Another will set out the cups. Another will create the posters and directional signs. Note how specialized labor kicks in. One kid doesn't have to do a little of everything.

That's inefficient. Tasks are spread out, and as the kids become highly skilled at the particular function they were assigned, both efficiency of effort and production soars. So, there we have it. Starting capital plus raw resources plus specialized labor produces large numbers of finished products ready for customers ~ in the kids' case, thirsty customers.

In his fourth book, Smith argues against any type of constraint against free trade.

Won't it be terrible for the kids if some bullies came over from across the street and said that some of the customers were actually from a different neighborhood, and if our kids want to sell lemonade to those customers, they will have to cut the bullies in for some of the profits? Or if some other bullies simply ran over, muscled in and took over the stand? Anything that would hamper our kids in any way with the selling of their lemonade to anyone passing by, no matter where they lived, would not be good for their profits, right?

That's the essence of Smith's argument in his fourth book. Capitalists, our lemonade kids in this instance, want the ability and right to safely sell their products wherever they want and to whomever they want, without any restrictions of any kind. That's Smith's argument against any type of constraints, or hindrances, against the marketing and selling of goods. Simply put, it's not good for business. Capitalists want free, protected markets from which they can safely pull their profits. But, our kids have a problem. Who's going to protect them, and their profits, from the threatening bullies?

In his fifth book, Smith says that's where government steps in, with legitimacy.

For instance, the kids might pay one of their parents, or probably an older sibling, to guard them and their lemonade stand from the bullies. Remember, in Capitalism, a most fundamental assumption is that government exists to protect private rights, especially safeguarding capital and profits. Smith argues in his fifth book that government taxes are actually good for business. In return for the taxation, private business can expect, and demand, that government protects their enterprises. Of course, in this vein, Smith also argues that taxes should be progressive, i.e., the more the profits, the more the taxes. Makes sense, doesn't it?

Smith also points out that since government's primary mission is to safeguard Capitalism together with its sacred rights to private ownership ~ that governments should be essentially limited, or restricted, to just that purpose. Hence the capitalist argument for limited government.

It's quite a manuscript, and in his tome *The Wealth of Nations* Adam Smith lays out the basic structure of Capitalism, wherever it may be practiced today. Capitalist investors pool their resources. They purchase raw materials. They use specialized labor to convert raw materials into finished products. They market and sell those products to whomever and wherever they can. They expect government to tax them, and in return, to primarily use those taxes to protect capitalistic enterprises. When it works right, according to Smith's vision, capital investors make lots and lots of money.

And, that's exactly how it works today. Whether it's gasoline in our cars, automobiles in our driveways, or clothing and food in the supermarkets, capitalist investors are behind all of it. They create a company by issuing stock, they purchase raw materials, they mix in some specialized labor, and they come up with marketable products. They expect no obstacles to their marketing and selling of their products, and they expect their government to protect and safeguard those expectations. Practically everything we buy or consume today comes to us via this capitalistic structure and mechanism.

Path to the Sacred Goal

Of course, there are other quite popular ways to play the capitalist game besides the manufacturing and selling of finished goods. Let's explore three of the more popular ones.

One does not necessarily have to invest capital in a start-up business plan. In ongoing businesses, there are always investors who would like to "get out" for whatever reasons and appreciate someone buying them out of their stock position. Hence, of course, the stock markets. Many investors seek to make their fortune in the buying and selling of stock positions in various companies. Their interest is not necessarily in whether the business actually thrives or not, but rather if they can buy someone else's stock position low, and turn around and resell that stock position to another party for a nice profit.

There is a certain element of gambling to that approach, and the buying and selling of existing stock positions has become quite complex. In this approach to increasing personal wealth, huge fortunes have been made, and of course, huge fortunes have been lost. Stock market dynamics are volatile by nature, and things can happen in the relative blink of an eye.

An investor playing the secondary stock markets has to be extremely focused and on top of what's happening.

Then there are those queasy souls who don't like to manufacture and sell finished products, and neither do they like to play the stock markets. They want to invest in something more "down to earth," as they would say. Huge fortunes have been made in the purchasing, development, renting, and selling of real estate. It tends to be a slower approach to increasing personal wealth, but it doesn't necessarily carry the risks of playing the up-and-down stock markets. One can own and manage rental real estate alone, or together with other investors. It is a popular approach to building capital wealth, for those who find the volatility of stock markets distasteful.

Then there are those other poor souls who want to make it big too, but don't have any money to invest, whether in a business, or in stocks, or in real estate. What are they to do?

Justin Bieber just showed us, didn't he! A Canadian teenager raised in limited means by a single parent, Justin discovered that he enjoyed singing and playing musical instruments. His Mom posted a home video of Justin playing and singing on a popular social website, and the rest is history. Justin's monetary wealth went from zero to multimillions overnight. But, what was his capital investment, if he didn't have any money to start with in the first place?

Remember how we chose to define "capital" earlier? "Material possessions, personal gifts and talents, personal energy, and personal time." Today's superstars might not start with money, per se, but they do discover and do put to good use their own personal gifts, energy, and time. An intelligent mix of one's personal gifts, energy and time can yield tremendous capitalistic profits.

Many of us fritter away our talents, energy and time. The superstars don't. They know what their talents are. They spend untold hours practicing and perfecting those talents. They pour all their personal energy into pursuing their goals. While most of us squander away our own time watching TV or spending idle time with friends, the superstars are hard at work developing themselves. That's their capital ~ a highly disciplined person capable of turning their talents and commitment and practice into monetary profits. Again, huge fortunes are made overnight.

These superstars exist in all walks of life. The creative arts. Sports. The corporate world. Mass media. The list goes on and on. Just watch the TV and you'll see the superstars parade across the screen. For these people, their starting capital was themselves ~ their native gifts, their personal energy, and the personal time they put into investing in themselves and the development of their gifts and their goals. In a sense, they treated *themselves* as a business with the goal to turn capitalistic profits. One doesn't always have to have start-up money to make profits. Wealth comes in many forms. The common capitalistic requirement is that the starting wealth be private, and that the profits arising from the manipulation of that starting wealth be protected.

Societal Stratification

Let's see where we stand now. We have reviewed capitalist assumptions, types of personal wealth, the capitalistic structure and dynamic, and different examples of capitalistic profiteering in today's capitalistic world. We know that in Capitalism, an individual's value is measured by their personal wealth, or lack of it. What about our other questions? In a capitalist philosophy-of-life, how is the individual taught to view others?

Let's pretend that we are an individual, capitalistic investor. What are the different ways that we could view another individual?

We might view them as a possible partner, to the degree that we would consider them useful and trustworthy. Or, if not as a partner, then perhaps as a profit center, i.e., a consumer of our goods ~ maybe we can sell them something. If not as a partner or as a customer, we might view them as a competitor, if they are selling something to others that competes with our own products. If not as a partner or consumer or competitor, then perhaps as cheap labor in our own factories. That's four different ways an individual in a capitalist culture can view another individual as either useful or important to the investor. Of course, those others too poor in personal resources to fit into any of those four categories have no place in a capitalistic culture. In Capitalism, they are known as the "unnecessary poor."

The line between self and other seems sharp and clear, and is generally defined by utility. Is there a bridge over that divide? Perhaps there is, in a true partnership, to the degree that the partners are loyal to each other, and don't start competing amongst themselves. Otherwise, the line between self and other is impassable. One uses the other to advance one's own goal, the maximization of one's individual, personal wealth.

How about our most pressing question? Can Capitalism bring about a utopia here on Earth?

Stance Toward Earthly Utopia

It's apparent that utopia, for an individual capitalist, would be to own everything on the planet ~ the true, or extreme, maximization of individual wealth. Of course, that would leave everyone else disfranchised and poor. The capitalist would be in its own capitalistic heaven, but everybody else would be in a capitalistic hell, so to speak. We are looking for a utopia for everyone, not just a few. Because of that, Capitalism doesn't seem to have much to offer in the way of a universal utopia. Despite its awesome ability to produce large amounts of exciting consumer goods within an unbeatable economy of scale, Capitalism offers the concept of utopia only to the extremely wealthy.

Of course, even if Capitalism was to be able to bring a utopia to lots and lots of people, it would be meaningless. Given the environmental degradation caused by the manufacture of its innumerable products, the utopia would be short-lived. Humanity would have long since joined the dinosaurs in the extinction parade, leaving all their material goodies as useless trash on the surface of the planet.

Together ~ thru the challenges of today ~

~ and into the promises of tomorrow

Expressions of Consciousness
2nd book of the *Bubbles of Consciousness* book series

Chapter 5 – Christianity

As one of the major philosophies-of-life, Christianity brings to humanity a powerful message of both love and sacrifice. Being the largest worldwide religion in terms of sheer numbers of believers, adherents can be found on all of the world's continents. Countless people view Christianity as their major expression of collective human consciousness, and strongly feel that it should be the accepted conventional thinking for everyone. Because of that strong feeling, Christianity has an aggressive missionary element about it, and Christian missionaries can be found everywhere actively promoting the message of Christianity and inviting non-believers to become believers.

Christianity has interesting historical roots, and we'll start our review of Christianity by looking at these roots. These historical roots also happen to contain Christianity's deepest founding assumptions.

Grounding Assumptions

Christianity views humanity's fundamental nature as both evil and corrupt. That happens to be a very negative view of humanity. How did Christianity come to that negative view? The answer lies within Christianity's most sacred assumptions ~ acceptance of the old Hebrew story of the Garden of Eden.

It goes somewhat like this. A supreme being, God, builds a paradise ~ a utopia so to speak ~ called the Garden of Eden. That same supreme being then creates the first man and woman, and places them in this paradise of beauty and perfection. So far, everything is good. Then that same supreme being places a certain tree in the middle of the Garden of Eden, commanding the first man and woman not to eat of the fruit of that special tree. They are allowed to eat the fruit of all the other trees, but not of the tree in the middle. Of course, they immediately eat some of the forbidden fruit. Anyone who has raised children knows how that works.

Then the supreme creator gets mad and tosses them out of the Garden of Eden, and curses them and all of their descendants to endure lives of misery and hardship, never to be allowed back into the Garden of Eden. When they die, they are destined to go straight to another place of misery and hardship, called Hell, there to be tormented forever because the first man and woman disobeyed the command not to eat the fruit of that special tree placed in the middle of paradise.

That's the first grounding assumption in Christianity ~ that humanity is basically of a corrupt and evil nature because of that original disobedience in the Garden of Eden.

The second grounding assumption is that all of humanity, descendants of the first man and woman, are equally corrupt and evil, because they are all born of the same nature as the first man and woman.

The third grounding assumption of Christianity is that all these wicked humans are destined to go straight to Hell when they die, because all of them have been barred from returning to paradise, the Garden of Eden.

Together, these three grounding assumptions constitute the bedrock upon which the teachings of Christianity are built. One cannot declare oneself to be a Christian unless one unquestioningly accepts this story, known among Christians as the story of the "original sin."

Sacred Goal

Of course, given these grounding assumptions, it is not difficult to fathom what Christianity's sacred goal is. Every Christian wants to find a way to avoid the original curse condemning all of humanity to Hell. Upon death, every Christian wants to go to a place of bliss, instead of to a place of torment and suffering, i.e., Heaven instead of Hell. It is tantamount to wanting to return to the Garden of Eden, from which all of humanity had been banished.

The question is ~ how to do this, when the original curse was so all encompassing?

Sacrifice

That's where the concept of sacrifice comes in. It's an old concept, found in most of humanity's early cultures. Generally speaking, the sacrifice, or slaughter, of animals was designed to appease angry gods, the same gods held responsible for humanity's sufferings. In times of great peril, even humans were sacrificed to the angry gods, hoping to turn the wrath of those gods away from humanity. Sacrificing animals and humans to angry gods is found so widespread among humanity's early cultures that it can almost be considered a universal cultural practice during those earlier times. Whatever the calamity or misfortune might be, sacrifice to angry gods was the socially approved method to attempt to minimize or neutralize humanity's enduring hardships.

Christianity is no different. It too turns to sacrifice to appease its angry supreme being. However, it puts an interesting and unique twist on the strategy of sacrificing to appease angry gods. Instead of sacrificing to the supreme being, it sacrifices the supreme being itself.

How's that? Let's take a look. This is where Christianity distinguishes itself from other expressions of conventional thought.

Seems that Christianity's supreme being, God, decides that it really does love the humanity that it had created, and wants to save humanity from the terrible curse it had placed upon humanity, i.e., predestination to an eternity of suffering in Hell. So, that supreme being decides to incarnate itself within a human form, known as Jesus. Jesus then teaches the importance of love to humanity. This message of love is not well received by humanity, and Jesus is tortured and put to a cruel death. Jesus dies, but miraculously three days later comes back to life and ascends back up into heaven. That torture and death of God incarnate in a human form is viewed as the ultimate sacrifice, and for humanity is seen as opening a door back into paradise. Let's explore all of this in a little more detail.

The Christian supreme being, God, is appreciated as a "Trinity of One." In other words, the Christian God has three distinct aspects even though it is understood that there is only one supreme being. There is God the Father; that's the aspect of God that started the whole thing in the first place as spelled out in the story of the Garden of Eden. There is God the Son; that's the aspect of God that became incarnate in the human form known as Jesus that was tortured and sacrificed, only to rise from the dead three days later. Then there's God the Holy Spirit; that's the aspect of God that is supposed to be found within any human who has hope to return to paradise upon death, instead of going straight to Hell. That's salvation, from a Christian perspective.

For any individual human, Christian salvation is triggered by the unquestioning acceptance of all of the foregoing. To be a "saved" Christian, one must accept, without question, (1) the story of the Garden of Eden, (2) the narrative of the life of Jesus, and (3) that God as Jesus has the power to grant salvation (escape from Hell) to anyone who believes in him. The driving assumption is that anyone, in this particular case Jesus, who can be tortured and cruelly killed only to come back to life three days later, must have absolute power over life and death, and consequently the power to overcome the original curse and reopen the gates of paradise to those who honor his life and sacrifice. Christians view the life, sacrifice, resurrection, and ascension of Jesus as the most important event in human history.

According to Christian teachings, anyone who does not believe in Jesus still goes straight to Hell upon death, as directed by the curse arising from the original sin in the story of the Garden of Eden.

Those who do accept and believe in the story of the Garden of Eden and in the life and sacrifice of Jesus are said to be "saved" (from Hell) and filled with the God as the Holy Spirit. This "indwelling" of God the Holy Spirit within an individual is understood to be the sign of Christian salvation. According to Christian teachings, there is no other way to be saved from the terrible fate awaiting all other humans, as taught in the story of the Garden of Eden.

Christianity teaches that either you believe in Jesus and go to Heaven, or you don't believe in Jesus and go straight to Hell.

Sacred Text

The sacred text for all Christians is known as the Bible, divided into two parts, the Old Testament and the New Testament. The Old Testament chronicles the Garden of Eden story, and suggests that a savior will come to humanity sometime in the future to save humanity from the terrible curse arising from the original disobedience in the Garden of Eden. The New Testament chronicles the life of Jesus as that promised savior, and the founding of the early Christian church based on his life and teachings.

The New Testament also chronicles the Christian belief that sometime later God as Jesus will come back to earth at the end of time, sweep away all remaining evil and wickedness, and establish paradise right here on earth ~ Heaven or the Garden of Eden, depending on how you look at it. Those swept away as evil and wicked will still be permanently exiled to an existence of eternal suffering in Hell, with the "saved" others remaining in the newly established paradise on earth.

Rituals

Christians celebrate the life of Jesus thru several life events. Christmas celebrates Jesus' birth. Baptism by water celebrates the entry of the individual into the Christian community. The Lord's Prayer condenses the teachings of Jesus, further elaborated in his celebrated Sermon on the Mount. The Eucharist celebrates Jesus' last meal before he was crucified and killed. Easter celebrates Jesus' rising from the dead three days after being killed. Every seventh day of the week, Christians come together in church gatherings for community worship, as taught by Jesus. And of course, there is always the strong missionary element, spreading the teachings of Jesus to those who are not yet Christians.

The predominate symbol of Christianity is the cross, known the world over. It was on a Roman cross that Jesus was crucified until dead. For all Christians, the cross as a symbol is a constant reminder of the suffering and ultimate sacrifice of Jesus, together with his resurrection and his presumed ability to grant Christian salvation to anyone who believes in his life, his teachings, his suffering, his sacrifice, and his resurrection and ascension back into Heaven.

Path to the Sacred Goal

Now that we have the philosophy-of-life known as Christianity somewhat worked out, let's look at our guiding research questions.

What is Christianity's stance toward self, the individual? As we have seen, the presumption is that the individual is evil and wicked, and is predestined to stay that way unless the individual accepts, without question, the story of the original sin in the Garden of Eden, and believes that Jesus has the power to lift that original curse off the individual.

What is Christianity's stance toward other? How is the individual, or self, supposed to view and treat other? All others are in the same position as self, i.e., evil and wicked unless saved by Jesus. However, even though others may be evil and wicked ~ self is taught to treat other with love and forgiveness, emulating the life of Jesus. This is known in Christianity as "turning the other cheek" ~ answering evil with good. It can be thought of as a sort of "sacrificial" love ~ sacrificing, or giving up, one's own innate impulse to retaliate and instead greeting the violator with love and forgiveness.

According to Christianity, what is the nature of the boundary between self and other? That position is extremely clear. All individuals start existence with wicked and evil natures. However, those who accept the teachings of Christianity are considered "saved" and bound for Heaven, while those who do not accept the teachings of Christianity are considered wicked and evil, and bound for everlasting torment in Hell. The boundary between self and others is extremely well defined, and only crossed over by accepting the teachings of Christianity.

Stance Toward Earthly Utopia

What is Christianity's stance toward a utopia on earth? Again, the teachings are very clear. Christians are waiting for God as Jesus to come back to establish Heaven on earth by sweeping all remaining wickedness and evil permanently into Hell so that earth again becomes the paradise it was as the Garden of Eden.

Unfortunately, it is a historical fact that Christians have been waiting more than two thousand years for Jesus to come back to reestablish a utopia on earth. Given our pressing needs of the moment, we cannot afford to wait another two thousand years for someone to come and save humanity from its pressing problems. By that time, humanity will have been environmentally flushed off the planet. Despite Christianity's deeply profound message of love and selfless sacrifice, it is not necessarily a good candidate for bettering humanity's present situation. Humanity needs something much more immediate. Waiting is no longer an option.

Chapter 6 – Communism

What we term *modern state communism* has affected so many people in today's world that it deserves to be treated as a major philosophy-of-life, or expression of collective human consciousness ~ and very much a strongly pronounced type of collective conventional thinking. Proposed as a critical alternative to today's prevailing economic capitalism, modern state communism can be expected to offer values, goals and means quite opposed to those held sacred by capitalism.

Various types of simple communism, or communal living, have always existed from the early mists of time, and can be expected to continue to be attractive to any number of peoples in the future. In reviewing this philosophy-of-life, we will need to be careful to distinguish between historic, elemental communal living and the modern state capitalism that we hear about so much today.

Community

The very essence of communism ~ whether elemental historic or modern state ~ is found in the collective, group ownership of everything. Individuals own nothing, not even their personal exertions or thoughts. It all belongs to the group. From the Latin, the root word "communis" means exactly that, i.e., that everything is shared and belongs to everyone in the group. No personal ownership ~ no personal rights. The group is all-important. The only rights that an individual may have are the temporary rights assigned to it by the group. The group is supreme.

Early hunting groups of prehistoric humans can be fancied to be just like that.

Imagine a group of desperate hunters in prehistoric times chasing after some really big, attractive game. It would not be acceptable for an inferior or inexperienced member of the hunting party to insist on clutching to himself the best spear in the group, so he could make the throw himself for an implausible shot at personal glory. Instead, he would immediately pass that best spear to the best hunter in the group, or the one in the best position to take the best shot. In that way, the best spear in the group really belongs to the group, and not to an individual, and automatically goes to the hunter in the best position to make a successful kill for the group.

Today, good basketball teams mirror that same group dynamic. No player is expected to "hog" the shot for personal glory, or think of it as "his" ball. Instead, he is expected to quickly get the basketball to the player in the best position to make the basket for the team. The basketball is expected to go instantly from the player who has it to the player who is in the best position to use it. Basketball teams where the individual players set aside their personal glory for the good of the team are usually the teams that rack up the victories. Teams beset by members quarreling over or competing for the basketball are sure losers. The same goes for most other team approaches to collective goals.

One doesn't't have to go all the way back to hunting and gathering tribal groups to find instances of simple communism.

Many religions, in their formative years, start with some sort of communal structure. Attempts at utopian societies have been made all over the world thru-out time. The driving essence is the same. Each individual contributes as much as it possibly can to the group, working hard to help support and sustain the group. All individual production is automatically owned by the group, not by the individual laboring at the task. In turn, the group takes care of the individual, making sure that individual needs are met.

Grounding Assumption

Modern communism captures this ageless communal civil structure with the following jingle ~ "from each according to his ability; to each according to his need." That's pure elementary community and incipient communism. The commune comes first, and in turn it takes care of the individual. This is the unquestioned, or sacred, assumption underlying any type of communism, or communal living.

Sacred Goal

Modern state communism embraces this pervading philosophy. However, modern state communism is far more aggressive in its applications, and directs its efforts at shunting aside today's prevailing capitalism, usually at the macro, or sovereign, nation level.

It accepts primitive communism's view that everyone should be treated equally in all aspects of human life, and consequently, views its highest and most sacred goal as bringing about a truly classless worldwide society where everyone is really treated the same ~ from each according to his ability, to each according to his need. In other words, no rich and poor, no powerful and weak, no educated and uneducated. Modern state communism wants all members of the group treated exactly the same on all aspects of human existence, whether it is power, wealth, or opportunity.

It views today's prevailing capitalism as riddled with social classes. Rich versus poor. Powerful versus weak. Educated versus uneducated. Franchised versus disfranchised. Modern state communism, in its quest for a truly classless human society where everybody is helping take care of everybody, wants to eradicate capitalism with its obvious and well-known social classes. Modern state communism views today's capitalism as its very antithesis not only in philosophy, but also in application and desirability.

How does modern state communism propose to eradicate today's prevailing capitalism? How does it propose to bring about a truly classless worldwide communist society, where everybody is not only treated the same but is actually the same on all social counts?

Path to the Sacred Goal

Two men, Karl Marx and Friedrich Engels, thought they knew how it could be done, and actually put their ideas and proposals into writing, authoring texts such as the *Communist Manifesto*, their classic treatise *Capital*, and the *Principles of Communism*. In these texts, Marx and Engels not only propose to eradicate today's prevailing capitalism, but propose exactly how to go about it. Let's take a look.

To set the stage for their proposal, Marx and Engels start by defining human history as an unbroken flow, or progression, of class struggle. A struggle between the powerful and the weak. A struggle between those who control others and those who are controlled by others. A struggle between those who have lots of things and those who have nothing ~ the haves and the have-nots. For Marx and Engels, human history is simply the seamless narrative of continuous struggle between opposing social classes.

A good example from ancient times would be the two definitive social classes of ancient Rome. The determinant was simple. One was either a "freeman" or one was a "slave." If one was a freeman, one could own things, including slaves, and exercise one's voice in social matters through public voting mechanisms. If one was a slave, one owned nothing, and had absolutely no voice in social matters. The most momentous event that could take place in the life of a Roman slave was to be granted one's freedom. It was tantamount to passing from one world to another, each the opposite of the other. As a freeman, one could make decisions for oneself; as a slave, one could make no decisions, not even for oneself. That's why the concept of freedom was so cherished in ancient times. With freedom, one was truly a "person." Without freedom, one was a social "nothing." Roman history is rife with accounts of slaves trying to become something, only to be put down and kept down by freemen, always by the prevailing law of the day, and many times violently. Roman freemen were not about to dilute their social prerogatives with the large slave community. These were the defining social classes in ancient Roman society. Freemen versus slaves. That lasted about a thousand years, give or take.

The next thousand or so years were dominated by medieval culture. Again, two disparate social classes defined medieval society ~ noble versus peasant. Nobles could accept grants of land from the reigning monarch. Nobles could become knights and heroes in war. Nobles could think and act for themselves, as long as they didn't displease or threaten their king. Nobles went on the game hunt, whilst peasants tilled the backbreaking soil. Peasants had very few rights, and could only do what their master allowed them to do. Peasants never took part in decision making. They only took and carried out orders from the nobles, and were threatened with immediate violence if they failed to perform. Peasants who tried to act "nobly" were deemed to be "putting on airs," and were harshly put "back into their place." It was considered scandalous for one of noble rank to socialize with ~ much less marry ~ a "commoner." Again, the social classes were very well defined by either birth, marriage or knighthood, and the noble class was not at all eager to dilute their own social prerogatives with the peasantry. Nobles versus peasants. That too lasted about a thousand years.

Then, according to Marx and Engels, along came capitalism, replacing the medieval social classes with new social classes of its own. Nobles were replaced by "capitalists." Peasants were replaced by "wage laborers."

How did that happen? It seems that two distinct trends took place at about the same time.

First, properties held in trust slowly became thought of as private holdings.

How's that? During the medieval period, royal sovereigns, title owners to all the land in their kingdom, would hand out fiefs, or land grants, to nobles who needed to be rewarded for some service to the crown. What was really handed over to the noble was the "use" of the land, not the land itself. It was understood that the land could, and would, revert back to the crown any time that the crown became displeased with the noble. Otherwise, the noble was expected to show its appreciation for the land grant by paying taxes to the crown, and providing provisions and warriors to the crown as the crown requested. The land use grant was inheritable, so if the noble still enjoyed the crown's pleasure when the noble died, the noble's heirs could take over the fief as long as they held to the original arrangement, e.g., paying taxes to the crown, and providing provisions and warriors to the crown as and when the crown requested.

As time passed and successive fief inheritances took place, the new fief holders started thinking of the land as their own, and no longer as actually held in fief trust for the crown. Royal dynasties that became politically weak also contributed to this psychological conversion process. The upshot was that individual nobles with fief land grants began to think of themselves as individually rich, and land wealth became concentrated in the hands of the nobility, who now thought of their lands as "private," and not as "trust lands." Peasants toiling for the nobility were left out of the arrangement, since they were considered to "belong" to the land and to whoever held the fief to it, just as any animals or crops on the land were considered to belong to the land and included in the original fief land grant.

Second, the industrial revolution took place. For the industrial revolution to thrive, it needed new social classes. Nobles hunting game in the forests or fighting wars amongst themselves were useless. Peasant toiling to raise primitive crops was equally useless. What the industrial revolution needed was a controlling social class with the private wealth to put together large industrial corporations, and a controlled working class willing to move to the industrial sites and work for a small wage. Hence, the noble class faded away and the capitalist class took its place. Peasants moved from the countryside to the industrial cities to work in the factories as hourly wage labor.

That's the situation Marx and Engels say that we have today ~ capitalists versus wage laborers. Still the same old ageless struggle between social classes ~ just with new definitions and new faces. Marx and Engels intend to put an end to this ageless class struggle. How? Let's see. Their proposal happens to be twofold.

Evolutionary Prognosis

Their proposal is that since capitalism is such a wonderful economic vehicle for churning out lots and lots of consumer goods, eventually too many goods and products will become available for purchase for the number of consumers out there. Their term for this development is *surplus goods*. Because of bloated inventories, prices will eventually weaken, and consumers will be able to pick up things for next to nothing. Of course, this will weaken capitalist profits, and in turn, weaken capitalism itself. Eventually capitalism will simply fade away, leaving consumers with oceans of goods and products.

With everyone in the new "land of plenty," classless communism will become the natural social order, with no one person working for another person. Everyone, in this land of endless goodness and supply, will freely direct their efforts toward the common good, knowing that they will never personally need or want again because capitalism has permanently removed personal need and want thru surplus production.

Marx and Engels argue that this will be the natural social evolution from capitalism to classless communism, i.e., as products go to surplus. As in any kind of natural evolution, it can take time, and no one can predict exactly when it will actually happen. Therein lies the rub ~ for Marx and Engels.

Violent Alternative

Marx and Engels weren't interested in waiting for the social "evolutionary process" to morph class-bound capitalism into classless communism. They wanted to see it happen immediately. They wanted to give history a push, or a shove, in that direction. Their proposal for doing that is rather fascinating in its approach.

Borrowing from the pages of human history and ageless class struggle, they actually proposed a new class-structured society ~ professional revolutionaries as the controlling social class and laboring workers as the controlled social class. Their arguments for this approach are rooted in both social psychology and capitalistic marketing.

Marx and Engels advance the line-of-thought that wage laborers in a capitalistic society are so psychologically ingrained into the capitalistic class system that they don't really know or understand what their real social position is. Capitalism's countless consumer products bedazzle the senses. Remote possibilities of becoming part of the rich, capitalist class beguile the mind. Marx and Engels suggest that the laboring wage class in a capitalist society is so bedazzled and beguiled by capitalism's charms that it will senselessly defend capitalism, even though its members are really oppressed by it. It is as if the laboring wage class is so completely bewitched by capitalism's offerings that they are in a deep psychological coma, completely oblivious to the real oppression of their laboring social class.

Marx and Engels have an answer for that ~ proposed as temporary ~ professional revolutionaries as a new controlling social class and laboring workers undergoing re-education as the new controlled social class.

The idea is that a class of professional revolutionaries, thru violent revolution, will overturn capitalism suddenly, bloodshed notwithstanding. Then, while they hold their new social order in trust for the proposed pure communist society, they will re-educate the working class, removing any capitalistic inclinations harbored in the worker's mind, and replacing those inclinations with new thought processes appreciative of the communistic proposal, and also appreciative of what the professional revolutionaries are doing for them, the laboring class. When the professional revolutionaries feel that the laboring class is fully ready to become true communists, then the professional revolutionaries will be able to step down as the trustees of society and allow the laboring class to manage the new communistic society themselves. Then, a pure classless communistic society will ensue.

In the meantime, of course, the professional revolutionaries will manage things on behalf of the working class, seizing all private property and rights in the name of their new society and intensely grooming the workers for true communism.

From the perspective of the professional revolutionaries, violent revolutions all around the world are the expectation, and the vehicle by which natural social evolution can be hurried. Without violent revolution, one has to wait for the natural process of social evolution to slowly unfold and take place. As we have seen in our earlier examples, social evolution can take centuries, even millennia. Marx and Engels and their professional revolutionaries don't have that kind of patience.

Stance Toward Earthly Utopia

Now that we have the communist proposal somewhat pinned down, let's review modern state capitalism in view of our research guidelines.

Given its emphasis on absolute equality for all, we should not be surprised that communism teaches all of its members the very same thing ~ from each according to its ability, to each according to its needs. Every single citizen in a communistic society is expected to accept this principle without question, and devote every personal energy to supporting the group. In turn, the individual can expect that the group, the communal or communistic society, will make sure that all personal needs are met and taken care of, and that the individual will not be left wanting for anything.

However, in the temporary situation that Marx and Engels outlines, there can be a boundary between self and other ~ professional revolutionary (communist party member) versus worker undergoing re-education (non-party member). Workers being re-educated can easily breach the boundary by simply accepting and internalizing the teachings of modern state communism. By doing that, the individual can become a true communist, and a true and reliable member of the communist party holding society in trust for the coming pure communist society. Until that happens, the individual continues to undergo re-education, which is, of course, intent on removing any capitalistic inclinations harbored in the individual's mind, and replacing those inclinations with new thought processes appreciative of the communistic proposal.

What about the utopia that we seek? What is modern state communism's stance toward that?

Pure communism wants the very same utopia that we all desire. Plenty for all ~ no want or despair ~ equality on all counts. No one can have a problem with that. That's what utopia is really all about. Communism proposes that the utopia we seek can come about in two different ways ~ slow evolutionary development or quick violent attainment.

Unfortunately, neither approach is desirable for us. Given the pressing environmental issues threatening us, waiting for evolutionary progress is not a winner. We'll be long gone before social evolution can bring our utopia to us. Our environmental health is on the edge of the cliff right now, and must be addressed immediately ~ not within centuries or millennia. Right now, the only thing natural evolution might bring to us is environmental replacement by other species.

Change, or progress, thru violence is equally unacceptable, especially in a time when nations are possessed of nuclear weaponry capable of the ultimate worldwide destruction of humanity. A true utopia should not be founded in bloodshed and violence. A legacy of bloodshed and violence will ultimately shred anything forged by that particular approach. The true roots of a lasting utopia should be nourished by something that does not have any destructive elements about it. Wisdom, goodwill, togetherness ~ those elements would make much better foundations for a new utopia than the bloody slaughter of other human beings.

So, despite the wonderful vision that true communism holds out for us, the route that it offers to that vision renders it useless for our purpose. We need to get to our utopia fast, and without any more destruction than we have already inflicted on ourselves and on our environment.

Together ~ thru the challenges of today ~

~ and into the promises of tomorrow

Expressions of Consciousness
2nd book of the *Bubbles of Consciousness* book series

Chapter 7 – Confucianism

Confucianism brings together, in a very deliberate and structured way, the twin themes of ethics and community. As a major type of human conventional thinking, the Confucian message has influenced many other philosophies-of-life, both Eastern and Western. It seeks to purposely shape both individual and collective human thinking and behavior in order to strategically and peacefully bring about social harmony and goodwill. Due to both its situs and its historic worldwide influence, it is worthy of our examination as a notable expression of collective human consciousness.

Grounding Assumptions

Confucianism is based on three grounding assumptions, each equally important as the other two. It is upon these three all-important assumptions that Confucianism seeks to build a world of social harmony and well-being.

First, Confucianism assumes that humans are essentially good. This is an important premise. A certain number of other major philosophies-of-life start with the opposite assumption ~ that humans are essentially bad. However, Confucianism also accepts that even though humans are essentially good, they can stray from that goodness and fall into evil and wickedness. This can happen thru such things as happenstance, bad choices, and ignorance.

Second, Confucianism assumes that, even though humans are basically good but perhaps weak, humans can be strengthened thru proper teaching. The essence of the second assumption is that humans are "teachable," and that thru the correct instruction and cultivation of ethics and proper daily behavior humans can be improved and perfected into sage-like beings. This second assumption is also quite important, because given this assumption, humans are not necessarily seen as the helpless captives or victims of happenstance, bad choices and ignorance. Thru proper counsel and guidance, humans are considered able to rise above ordinary human fooleries to become the bastions of the perfect human society.

Third, Confucianism assumes that goodness, both at the individual and social levels, is worth dying for. Or, to put it another way ~ that righteousness within the individual and humaneness and respect toward others are more important than life itself. This is where we find the sacred in Confucianism. It would be better to die as a steadfast and wise sage than to live as a weak and foolish human. Mere physical survival of the individual is not seen as quite that important. Far more important is "how" the individual is living its life, and "how" it fits into surrounding society. Mere survival is secondary.

Sacred Goal

Given these three grounding assumptions, it is not difficult to appreciate that Confucianism has two interrelated goals, mostly directed toward the individual, with a sharp eye to the social. In pursuing the Confucian goal of building the perfect social edifice, individuals are viewed as the elementary building blocks of that perfect society.

The first goal in Confucianism is to develop the perfect individual. The perfect individual will demonstrate a certain three aspects of character and behavior.

First, the perfect individual will be a paragon of virtue and righteousness ~ a pillar of honesty and trustworthiness. Second, the perfect individual will display a benevolent humanity toward its fellow human beings ~ being kind and compassionate and thoughtful to others. Third, the perfect individual will be appropriately respectful of others, giving and showing true loyalty when socially expected or earned, as the social situation may dictate.

Any individual demonstrating mastery on all three of these counts is considered a sage, or perfected individual.

The second, and great, goal in Confucianism is to develop the perfect society ~ out of these perfected individuals, of course. Confucianism does not expect to bring about the perfect society by means of police enforcing legal dictates at the point of a gun. That approach brings with it violence, which usually brings more violence right behind it, in an upward spiraling sort of way. Instead, Confucianism seeks, so to speak, to put the police inside the individual.

Perfected individuals do not need laws and police enforcement since they are self-policed by their own perfection. They are paragons of virtue, kind to others, and respectful of their fellow human beings. Such people are self-monitoring, and in no need of external or outside policing. Instead of being controlled by fear of the gun, they are controlled by the fear of personal shame and losing face in front of others.

In Confucianism, social harmony does not come from enforced laws and prisons, but by individuals monitoring and controlling themselves thru proper education and development. Social control is internalized within the individual. It is not imposed upon the individual by outside police action. This way, the Confucian perfect society comes about congenially and peacefully, and not violently and at the cost of human conflict and suffering.

Path to the Sacred Goal

Therein lies the grounding assumptions and goals of the Confucian vision. The Confucian approach to those goals is, as can be expected, via the development and education of the individual, with certain social rewards for attainment and mastery.

The Confucian approach to developing the perfected individual is three-pronged. Let's explore them in a little more detail. The first approach can be thought of as the development of a moral center within the individual, the second approach as the development of a generalized humanity toward others, and the third approach as the development of a sensitivity to social position, or rank.

For the first approach in developing the perfected individual, the presence of a moral center within the individual suggests virtues such as dependability, honesty, integrity, justness, knowledge, righteousness, trustworthiness ~ i.e., ~ individual, personal "goodness." Thru proper instruction and absorption these virtuous concepts become so ingrained and internalized that a strong moral center is established within the individual. Morality is not relativized to the surrounding social situation; it is deeply centered within the individual and independent of any given social situation. No matter what kind of social situation the individual might find itself in, others will always find the individual without fail to be honest, full of integrity, just, knowledgeable, righteous, and trustworthy.

The moral center doesn't bend under outside pressure, nor does it lose its internalized integrity. The individual's morality is a rock-solid constant, regardless of the social situation. Because of this, social situations do not affect the individual's moral center. Rather, the individual with a strong moral center affects and impacts the social situation within which it finds itself ~ from moment to moment as time flows and carries the individual thru different and ever-changing social situations.

As philosophies-of-life go, Confucianism rather singularly points out that human speech is an extremely important facet of the social recognition of individual goodness. If a message is accidentally incorrect or misunderstood, the individual's personal goodness might not be duly recognized and appreciated, and the message coming from the one of perfected goodness could inadvertently be misleading to the listener.

There are many known problems in human communication. Let's look at a few of the better-known ones. Many words have multiple meanings ~ in all human languages around the globe. And, assumptions underlying the spoken message might be different on the part of the speaker and the listener. The jargon of the speaker might not be fully understood by the listener. The speaker might tiptoe around a delicate subject, not being willing to take the risk of offending the listener, and the listener in turn might misinterpret the true intent of the speaker. The spoken message might be affected by ego or emotional or personality filters on either the part of the speaker or the listener.

A common game to illustrate the rather undependable nature of human communication and language is to have one person quietly whisper a semi-complex message to another person, and so on down a line of subjects, whispering quietly and always from just one person in the line to just the next person in the line. It can be absolutely amazing how the messages received by the last person ~ say the 25th person at the end of the line ~ can so widely vary from the original message started by the 1st person at the head of the line. Playing this illuminating game can be an experience that stays with one for a long time.

Since, in the Confucian world-view, individual goodness is intended to be the building block of the perfect society, it is important that individual goodness be recognized and not clouded or obscured by human language issues. That is why Confucianism insists that human speech must be correct and precise, using concepts and terms that actually reflect the reality that is being talked about.

Think about it. A very honest person who is accidentally misunderstood due to human language problems could come across as a very dishonest person, notwithstanding how honest that person may really be. People do view and assess each other thru speech, and that is why for a person who has developed a strong moral center, speech must be absolutely clear and precise and true, and in no manner susceptible to misinterpretation.

For the second approach in developing the perfected individual, the development of a generalized humanity toward others suggests treating others fairly, as one would want to be treated oneself. Or, to put it another way, one would want to avoid treating others in any way that one would not want to be treated by others. It's simply the Golden Rule, found in some fashion in most, if not all, philosophies-of-life. It's probably the most core value in Confucianism, and interestingly enough, the bedrock for any long-lasting human group, whether the group is as small as a family or team, or as large as a great civilization.

Without fairness, meaningful human relationships cannot endure. Fairness is the cement that holds us peacefully together. Treating others fairly, as one would want to be treated, causes one to be perceived by others as humane ~ gentle, kind, and selfless ~ the exact opposite of what goes on in the primeval jungle.

This is the generalized humanity toward others that Confucianism is looking for within the perfected human.

For the third approach in developing the perfected individual, the development of a sensitivity to social position, or rank, suggests a respect for others guided by an appreciation for where others are positioned within society's ranking system. Social hierarchy becomes important. Sons and daughters are respected as offspring, fathers and mothers as parents, and managers as superiors. Not only does every possible social relationship calls for a certain code of behavior, or etiquette, but everyone occupies certain places in the social order. An individual may be an offspring, a parent, a subordinate, and/or a superior ~ all at the same time with respect to various other individuals. Each relationship calls for certain levels or types of respect, or decorum.

Of course, others, to trigger that respect from the individual, must themselves be respectable in the required degree. Superiors, even emperors, who do not demonstrate the appropriate moral center and generalized humaneness toward others that is appropriate to their social position ~ in turn are not entitled to the respect they could have had from those beneath them in the social pecking order. Reciprocity, in the Confucian world, is very important. Not only is it important to show the appropriate respect to others, but one must also behave in such a way as to be perceived by others as respectable and actually deserving of the respect that normally comes with one's own social station.

With these three developmental approaches toward shaping the individual ~ establishment of a moral center within the individual, a generalized humaneness toward others, and an appropriate respect for social status ~ Confucianism seeks to bring the individual to a sage-like perfection of character, worthy of being a building block of the sought-after perfect Confucian society.

Social Reciprocity

Given its focus on the social order, we should not be surprised that social relationships are very important in the Confucian world. If we think of perfected individuals as the building blocks of the perfect society, then we would think of social relationships as the cement that holds the building blocks together to establish the social edifice. Of course, in this analogy, the quality of the cement becomes highly important ~ it needs to have some very good "stickiness" in order to hold the building blocks together in place over very long periods of time.

In its desired social order, Confucianism seeks to ensure the "stickiness" of its social cement thru the establishment of potent social rituals ~ differing rituals, or codes of behavior and speech, for every single social relationship possible. It is thru these exacting and enduring social rituals that Confucianism attempts to maintain proper, hierarchal relationships and Confucian values within its smoothly functioning society. Because of this particular approach to maintaining social harmony and order, any society embracing Confucianism as the best philosophy-of-life to follow often becomes perceived as a highly ritualized culture.

However ~ one must remember ~ in viewing Confucianism, that rituals per se are not the essence of Confucianism. Rituals are a primary medium thru which Confucian values are maintained and safely transmitted over time from one generation to another. The four life events that are highly ritualized in the Confucian society are birth, reaching maturity, marriage, and death. We shouldn't be surprised that marriage ~ the only one of these four life events that talks directly to social relationships ~ is the most ritualized life event, broken down into six stages, each of which is highly ritualized within itself. These six stages are the proposal, the engagement, the dowry, the procession, the marriage/reception, and a special ceremony the next morning celebrating and honoring the importance of reciprocity in all social relationships.

Development of the perfected, sage-like individual is achieved mainly thru education ~ not merely education when the individual is young ~ but education throughout life. Life itself is viewed as a continuous process of education. If one is not learning something to bring about individual perfection ~ that is not good. Learning the art of "goodness" should be so important to the individual that other pursuits or appetites in life are viewed as distant and secondary.

Guiding Texts

There are many important texts in Confucianism used to promote the Confucian mind-set via lifetime education and learning. Some of the more important are the Four Books (Lun Yu, Chung Yung, Ta Hsueh, Meng Tzu) and the Five Classics (Shu Ching, Shih Ching, I Ching, Ch'un Ching, Li Ching). Of these nine texts, the Lun Yu, or *Analects of Confucius*, is considered the most important and sacred. It is thru these sacred texts and other supporting commentaries that Confucian values are taught and transmitted from generation to generation.

Immediate Rewards for Goal Attainment

Just as Confucianism rather singularly points out that human speech is an extremely important facet of the social recognition of individual goodness, it also rather singularly rewards the establishment of goodness within the individual. Many religions, or philosophies-of-life, support the desirability of goodness within the individual by promising special rewards in an afterlife ~ goodness goes to heaven; a lack of goodness goes somewhere else. Confucianism, which does not necessarily postulate the existence of a supreme deity or a heaven or a hell, takes a different and somewhat unique approach. It finds a different way to reward education and learning and the acquisition of well-rounded individual goodness.

For personal development toward individual goodness, Confucianism promises rewards in one's present live ~ one does not have to wait for death to collect. Confucianism sets up a vast system to test individuals for personal development, and the immediate reward is social advancement in the current lifetime. Getting ahead by being the offspring of so-and-so doesn't cut it. Meritocracy is the game to be played. Comprehensive exams are offered to all. Those who do well on the exams move upward in the social pecking order, and those who do not do well on the exams remain stuck where they are, regardless of their family ties. In this Confucian system, individual ability is rewarded, not family ties or descent. Instead of a particular gene pool being favored in the Confucian world, demonstrated individual ability and development are rewarded.

Obviously, this approach puts everyone in that society on an equal footing for social position and advancement, and it is extremely democratic in providing equal social opportunity to all. Remember, as we noted earlier, even emperors who do not demonstrate the appropriate moral center and generalized humaneness toward others that is appropriate to their social position will lose their entitlement to be honored and respected as an emperor.

Now that we have an idea of what Confucianism is about, let's see how it talks to our research guidelines.

Stance Toward Earthly Utopia

The Confucian approach to the individual is generally positive. Confucianism calls for demonstrated righteousness on the part of the individual, and also posits that the individual is basically good ~ and that through continuing education the individual can hone that basic goodness to the point of sage-like perfection. Continuing education is also valued as the means by which a naturally good individual can avoid slipping into less than good behavior. Continuing education is viewed as central to the development of the individual. A lack of continuing education is viewed as putting the individual at the risk of sliding downward from even one's innate basic goodness. It is as if the individual is viewed as born with a basically good nature, and appropriate ongoing education ~ or the lack of it ~ generally dictates where the individual goes from there. That is the Confucian vision of the individual.

Confucianism dictates that the individual demonstrates a generalized humaneness toward others, together with appropriate respect for the other's position in the social pecking order. This requirement for humaneness and respect toward others is paramount. However, if others ~ including even the high and mighty ~ do not demonstrate the humaneness and respect toward individuals that is appropriate to their position, they in turn lose the right to receive respect from the individuals around them. In this particular social dynamic, we again see the great importance of reciprocity in the Confucian society. To the degree that another approaches the individual with integrity, humaneness and respect, the individual is expected to respond with appropriate cooperation in like measure.

Obviously, in the Confucian world, there are social boundaries between the self and others, highly ritualized through detailed etiquette specific to the particular boundary, or relationship. Thru these rituals everyone knows their place in society, and the place of the others around them. Nevertheless, ritual and etiquette in the Confucian society are not necessarily a lifelong prison for the individual. Thru education and application one can advance in the social order ~ all the way to the top as a perfected sage. It is as if the Confucian social pecking order is a ladder, and one always knows one's own position and the positions of others on that ladder at any one time. However, thru appropriate education and application, one can climb that social ladder ~ or slide down the social ladder if one's personal development is lacking.

Whereas many philosophies-of-life posit a utopia after death, Confucianism is looking for social utopia right here and now ~ in one's present life. Confucianism assumes that a present-day utopia is very attainable here and now, as long as human beings ~ born naturally good ~ are further educated and developed to maximize that goodness to a point of perfection, both individually and socially. In the Confucian social utopia, individuals will be so perfected and sage-like that thought, speech and behavior will approach free-flowing poetic expression. Ongoing ritual, both verbal and nonverbal, will maintain the utopia over time. All will be steeped in valuable cultural memories and historic traditions. Politics ~ instead of being competitive and self-seeking ~ will be attuned to the needs of the community as a whole.

Given the Confucian approach to bringing about a social utopia here and now in our lives, it may very well have something to offer to us in our quest for a quick turnaround of our current perilous situation. Given our pressing environmental problems, we need and want solutions right here and right now.

Confucianism shares that approach to bringing about a utopian existence for all human beings. It too wants the perfect society right here and right now ~ peacefully ~ not violently.

Together ~ thru the challenges of today ~
~ and into the promises of tomorrow

Expressions of Consciousness
2nd book of the *Bubbles of Consciousness* book series

Chapter 8 – Daoism

One of the two major expressions of Chinese conventional thinkings, *Daoism* ~ or *Taoism* ~ has more than 400 million adherents today, mostly in China and South-East Asia, although adherents generally can be found all around the globe. It has been variously referred to as either a philosophy of life or a religion, and Daoism tends to somewhat percolate the collective consciousness of many other peoples who verbally profess other philosophies-of-life as their principal guide in how to live the good, or socially approved, life. Its primary sacred text ~ the *Dao-De-Jing* (*Tao Te Ching*) ~ is reputedly the second most translated text in the world.

Historically, even though occasionally Daoism has had a strong formal political and social presence, it is essentially a personal and meditative approach to living. Its earliest historic roots can probably be traced to ageless shamanism wherein a shamanistic practitioner enters so-called altered states of consciousness ~ perhaps ecstasies or trances ~ in order to gain entrance to a spirit world for the purpose of obtaining supernatural help with worldly problems.

Daoism has some interesting grounding assumptions somewhat unique in its recommended approach to thinking and behaving correctly, and living the good, or correct, life. We'll look at them carefully since they form the bedrock of the Daoist perspective.

Grounding Assumptions

The foremost claim in Daoism is that there is only one source and driving force for overall existence, or reality, or creation ~ "Oneness." It is known as the "Dao" ~ variously translated as the "way" or the "path" or the "principle" or the "road" or the "power." The Dao is transcendent, and because of that transcendent nature the Dao is essentially unknowable by ordinary human intellect. The Dao permeates all of creation, and consequently the Dao is immanent in everything, including every single living human being. While ordinary human intellect cannot understand the Dao in its absolute, or essential, transcendent nature, a human being can know the Dao thru its manifestations and creations ~ the day-to-day existence, or reality ~ that human beings find themselves experiencing.

The Dao is not static. It is dynamic, constantly reordering itself, or creation, with various manifestations, or forms, perpetually going in and out of manifest existence. It is as if human existence, or reality, is constantly being reordered out of some sort of elemental, chaotic pool. Or, another way to think about it is ~ that the primeval transcendent void, pure potentiality, is constantly becoming manifest as form, and then form is just as quickly dissolving back into pure potentiality, the primeval transcendent void.

It's a constant effervescent flux. Because of this grounding assumption, Daoists are fond of saying that the only constant that we should expect in human existence is change itself.

Since the Dao is immanent in all of creation, Daoists claim that consequently the Dao must be perfectly reflected in nature itself, and that in the natural order the Dao will be found to be unaffected, spontaneous in expression, timeless, essentially nameless, and absolutely indescribable. This grounding assumption that the natural order is most perfectly reflective of the Dao tends to lead to a rather relaxed, hands-off approach to day-to-day living in the Daoist world.

Given the foregoing grounding assumptions, the Daoist working assumption is that harmony, or Oneness, with the Dao will lead to joy and a good and long ~ possibly immortal ~ existence. Conversely, not being in harmony, or Oneness, with the Dao will lead to the opposite, i.e., a relatively not-so-good and shorter ~ rather mortal ~ existence.

Sacred Goal

The Daoist sacred goal is obvious. At a bare minimum ~ joyful ecstasies. Perhaps a very good and a very long life ~ maybe even immortality. All, of course, attainable to the degree that the individual is in harmony ~ or at one ~ with the Dao. Since one of the grounding assumptions of Daoism is that the Dao can be found most readily within the natural order, it is believed that the working goal is to truly reflect the natural order within oneself. That should bring about meaningful and lasting harmony and Oneness with the Dao.

Path to the Sacred Goal

Since Daoism is primarily a personal and meditative activity, we need to explore what an individual practitioner does in order to come into harmony and Oneness with the Dao ~ to reflect the natural order within oneself. Daoism happens to offer a well-known allegory to suggest the correct approach.

The term *wu-wei* signifies meeting aggressive action with soft, self-effacing non-aggressive action, i.e., with naturalness, spontaneity, creativity, and simplicity.

Think of water gently coursing down a small stream bed. As the water flows downward, whenever it meets an obstacle in its path, it doesn't get an attitude or fight with the obstacle or try to shove the obstacle out of its way. The water merely flows around the obstacle to get to where it wants to go. This is known to Daoists as "action without (deliberate) action" ~ acting immediately without personal ego or calculating thought. The water flows down the stream bed and handles any obstacles in its path just as an infant may react to a stimulus ~ again ~ naturally, spontaneously, creatively, and simply.

The Daoist practitioners in harmony and Oneness with the Dao will find themselves handling the course of a human life just like the flow of the water handles the course of the stream bed. No personal ego. No calculating thought. Just flowing thru life naturally, spontaneously, creatively, and simply as a child would handle its early years before being educated into local human culture by its caretakers and handlers. That's wu-wei ~ being in harmony and Oneness with the Dao.

Now, of course, that is all well and good, but it begs the question of "how exactly does one arrive at the mental state of wu wei?" The typical human mind is a jumbled composite of personal ego and analytic thought processes. Exactly how can the Daoist practitioner get past this swirling mix of self-serving emotion and calculating cognition to enter into the mental state of ageless and thoughtless wu-wei ~ natural, spontaneous action without deliberate thought?

Strategies

It happens that there are a number of concrete steps that one can use as goals in meditation to approach and achieve wu wei. Let's examine them one at a time. These are the concrete means used in Daoist meditation to achieve the sacred goal ~ wu-wei ~ harmony and Oneness with the Dao, thereby bringing to the Daoist practitioner joyful ecstasies and a good and a very long life, perhaps even meaningful immortality.

One of the concrete steps in the Daoist meditative exercise is to understand and appreciate the *Oneness* of creation, or existence. The concepts of yin and yang can be of assistance. Often thought of a theory of opposites, yin and yang can really best be thought of as correlates. Correlates are not really opposites, but rather "apparent" opposites that are actually related ~ and mutually and totally interdependent upon each other for their conceptual existence. Conceptually, we cannot have one without the other. Each opposite, in its own way, defines its correlative opposite. Let's look at an example that all of us can appreciate.

Due to the fact that our planet spins on its axis somewhat perpendicular to the plane of its orbit around our sun, all of us experience the phenomena known as day and night, often casually and readily thought of as opposites. Day is thought of as the opposite of night because there is plenty of sunshine, while night is thought of as the opposite of day because there is an absence of sunshine. However, the existence of one is dependent upon the existence of the other. The concept of day is dependent on the existence of the concept of night. If the sun was to shine continuously without any interruption, the interrelated concepts of day and night could not exist. Furthermore, each one carries the harbinger of the other within itself. Just as surely as night follows day, so does day follow night. Instead of being simply opposites, day and night are more like partners mutually dancing to an ever-cycling rhythm. That's why they are best thought of as correlates of the same one single phenomenon, just as the two distinctive faces of a coin are merely "opposite" ~ but really correlative ~ aspects of the same single coin spinning endlessly ~ just as the earth spins endlessly around our sun creating the appearance of night and day.

Our human existence is made up of "apparent" opposites. Male and female. Life and death. Good and evil. Loud and soft. Fragrant and foul. Tasty and nasty. Hard and pliable. Hot and cold. The list is endless. The Daoist practitioner understands and appreciates that ~ instead of a cycle of endless apparent opposites ~ what's really happening is that single phenomena, i.e., Oneness, are merely endlessly cycling their correlative aspects to our various perceptions leading us to jump to the hasty conclusion of the existence of hard and fast opposites. It's like a show. The Daoist practitioner appreciates that, in the human existence, appearances can be deceiving. To understand and truly appreciate the nature of the Dao and to be in harmony with it, one must get past apparent appearances and appreciate the actual "Oneness" realities causing the dances of the appearances of opposites.

Another of the concrete steps in the Daoist meditative exercise is to gain *detachment* ~ or to become detached from any one correlative aspect of any particular reality. That's rather easy to do once one gets comfortable with the concept of pervasive oneness. Let's take a look at it using our example of day and night.

Wouldn't it be silly for someone to say that they are so attached to either day or night that they wish it would be either day all the time or night all the time? That would be scary! If it became day all the time, we would end up burning to a crisp. If it became night all the time, we would end up freezing to death. It's the endless dance of day and night that keeps us so comfortable ~ sun-shinny day to be happily active, and dark night to catch that refreshing sleep. We'd have a global panic on our hands if someone suddenly announced that there would be no more day, or no more night! Our comfort and security rest in the knowledge that the dance of day and night will go on endlessly.

The Daoist practitioners appreciate all the dances of the opposites, so to speak, and carefully do not let themselves become attached to any one aspect. That is detachment ~ or enjoyment without attachment. Day is enjoyed for what it has to offer, and likewise, night is enjoyed for what it has to offer. The same goes for any other apparent dance of the opposites ~ whether male/female ~ life/death ~ good/evil ~ loud/soft or hot/cold ~ and so on endlessly. The understanding of the underlying Oneness of creation helps us stay detached from any one phenomenal aspect, and enjoy ~ without attachment ~ the entire fluxing cycle.

The ability to remain detached from any one correlative aspect of an underlying unity leads to *contentment*. Again, the example of day and night. One can be content during the night, knowing that day will soon follow. And, one can be content during the day, knowing that night will soon follow. Contentment leads to a steady calmness regardless of which correlative opposite is being manifested at the moment, and enhances harmony and oneness with the Dao.

The ability to remain detached from any one correlative aspect of an underlying unity also leads to *receptivity*. Receptivity means to be free from a judgmental mentality. Good and bad ~ like and dislike ~ start losing their significance. What's better? Day? Night? One really cannot say. They are simply correlative opposites of the same constant effervescent flux. It's not a matter of one being better than the other. They are simply correlative aspects that continuously cycle and flow into each other.

So now we have our Daoist practitioner ~ thru personal meditation ~ in mastery of Oneness, detachment, contentment, and receptivity ~ eternally enjoying the endless show of creation ~ unaffected, spontaneous in expression, timeless, essentially nameless, and absolutely indescribable. It's almost like being a young child again. That's wu-wei. That's harmony and oneness with the Dao.

Tactics

However, directed meditation can be challenging, and meditative goals elusive, given the almost psychotic busyness of the human mind. Thankfully, meditative aids are available for the want-to-be Daoist. Let's look at three meditative aids in particular.

The first aid to Daoist meditation has to do with nature itself. Remember that Daoism claims that the Dao is perfectly reflected in the natural order and process of things. Ergo, that makes nature itself the best teacher for the Daoist practitioner ~ much better than cultural understandings and learned discourses and obtuse analysis that can be way off base. Just the simple, insightful observation of how nature works ~ particularly its innumerable cycles. Think of the seasons. Reproduction. Evaporation and condensation. The cyclical movement of tectonic plates. Daoists suggest that if one observes nature in an open and non-critical manner, one can learn a lot about the Dao and how to be in harmony and in Oneness with it.

As one learns about the Dao by observing natural processes ~ keeping in mind that human beings are part of the natural order and thereby a microcosm of nature ~ one starts letting oneself flow with the Dao. Remember ~ emerging mastery of the principles of oneness, detachment, contentment, and receptivity starts allowing the active realization of unaffectedness, spontaneity, timelessness, namelessness, and existential transcendence ~ essences of the Dao. A true understanding of the natural order allows one to really "know thyself" ~ and eventually become in complete harmony and oneness with the Dao.

The Three Jewels

The second aid to Daoist meditation is known as the Three Jewels, or Three Treasures. They are worldwide hallmarks of the Daoist approach to living the proper life. Let's look at them one at a time. Compassion, or kindness. Moderation, or simplicity. Humility, or modesty. All three of them enhance the ability to quietly learn directly from nature instead of becoming befuddled by opinionated scholarly discourse. The Three Jewels do that by acting as active nutrients to the germination and development of a sense of Oneness within the Daoist practitioner. Let's start with compassion.

The first Jewel ~ compassion, or kindness ~ talks to benevolence, comfort, sympathy, generosity, mercy and all the other qualities we expect in a general sense of goodwill, or humanity. It implies, or connotes, a sense of community, or empathy, or oneness, with other human beings. To the degree that we feel somehow linked to the other, or one with the other, we feel safe in letting our guard down and expressing goodness. Conversely, if we have negative feelings toward the other, such as fear or hostility or violence, any sense of oneness with the other voids and we think of that other human as something very different from ourself. We feel the need to defend, and our guards go up. That is why the first Jewel encourages positive feelings toward others, such as compassion and kindness ~ because these positive sympathies engender feelings of Oneness within the Daoist practitioner.

The second Jewel ~ moderation, or simplicity ~ talks to self-control, restraint, naturalness, and the lack of extremes. It implies, or connotes, the acquisition of objects only for necessary utility, and not for flashy showiness in front of others. One's lifestyle should be reasonably simple, and definitely not flamboyant. When we start acquiring unnecessary objects, we start becoming other-minded and start worrying about other people stealing our collections. The more we collect, the more we fear. Ergo, the feelings of fear and hostility and violence to protect our things grow within us, voiding any development of the feeling of oneness with others. Conversely, the fewer objects we own the easier it is to develop a sense of oneness with others, because we have less reason to fear them taking our stuff. Worldly possessions ~ or to be more exacting, possessiveness, a psycho-emotional state ~ act as a barrier to an overall sense of Oneness.

The third Jewel ~ humility, or modesty ~ talks to humbleness, decency, reserve, and demureness. It implies, or connotes, the absence of ego pretensions and self-aggrandizement and any type of artificiality of personality. Toward others, we should not present any type of false or made-up persona, and toward others we should simply be what we really are. "What you see is what you get." When we start to manufacture a false persona to present toward others, we start thinking of others as something distinct and separate from ourselves that needs manipulating. That voids any sense of oneness with others. Other has become an object to exert influence upon ~ to control ~ so to speak. Controlling others, or exerting any kind of authority over others, threatens the development of a sense of oneness. By modestly being our natural selves, it is easier for the sense of oneness to start to emerge within.

These Three Jewels ~ goodwill toward others, simplicity of lifestyle, modesty of persona ~ act as nutrients to the germination and development of a sense of Oneness within the Daoist practitioner. And, in doing that, these Three Jewels assist the Daoist practitioner to become in harmony and Oneness with the Dao. The practice of these Three Jewels is extremely important in Daoist practice.

Why? Because they enable the Daoist practitioner to be in harmony and Oneness with the Dao not only during meditation, but also during the course of ordinary living ~ regardless of whatever outside situation may be swirling around the Daoist practitioner at any particular moment.

The third aid to Daoist meditation is one of the most famous texts in the world ~ the *Dao-De-Jing (Tao Te Ching)*. Wrote by the legendary figure Laozi ("ancient child"), the text talks about the nature of the Dao and how to come into harmony and oneness with it. An ancient poetic mix of metaphors and puzzling contradictions, the text attempts to discuss the transcendent when by its very nature the transcendent transcends the ability of human language to accurately discuss anything transcendent. That's why all the poetry, metaphors, allegories, and puzzling contradictions, and that's why lots of deep personal meditation and the assistance of a Daoist master may be of some help. The *Dao-De-Jing* is trying to convey concepts that really cannot be reduced to human language. Indeed, it's difficult to grasp what the *Dao-De-Jing* is trying to say unless the text is approached somewhat transcendentally. Of course, like any great historic text, the *Dao-De-Jing* has numerous commentaries, of which the most famous are perhaps the *Zhuangzi* and the *Daozang*. They too offer help in understanding the nature of the Dao and how to come into alignment with it.

Outside of these personal efforts, Daoism finds itself socially expressed in collective activities such as parades on certain holidays, martial arts, sacrifices, fasting, fortune telling, astrology and divination. However, one must remember that Daoism is essentially a personal exercise, and ultimately the Daoist seeker must come to grips with the Dao at an individual level. Daoism, in its collective expression, is often associated with the yin/yang symbol, although the yin/yang symbol is also used by other systems of belief.

Stance Toward Earthly Utopia

Now that we have somewhat pinned down what Daoism, or Taoism, is all about, let's see how it talks to our research questions.

Daoism says that the individual is a microcosm of the universe, and of course, that means that everything in the universe, in a micro sense, can be found within the individual. That's what Daoism is all about. Daoism wants the individual to perfectly reflect the natural flow within, and in doing so, come into harmony with the Dao and "flow with the flow." Flowing with the flow ~ or being in relaxed harmony and Oneness with the Dao ~ yields to the individual a good, joyful existence and possibly even immortality.

As far as how the individual should treat other human beings ~ that's where Daoism's Three Jewels, or Three Treasures, comes in. One should approach others with compassion and kindness and goodwill. One should live moderately, and not flaunt one's wealth to others. One should be modest and unassuming, and not barricade oneself from others or attempt to control others with manufactured personas or inflated egos. The individual should make sure that all its relationships with others are characterized by goodwill, moderation, and natural humility.

Since Daoism views all that exists as part of the natural order, all human beings are part of the same natural order with no hard and fast boundary between. All are either (1) with the Dao, or (2) attempting to harmonize with the Dao, or (3) not in oneness with the Dao. Depending on the status of the individual's relationship with the Dao, individuals are living either good lives, or not-so-good lives, or somewhere in between.

Given Daoism's hands-off approach to manipulating or controlling others, the best thing any one individual can do to help another is to simply be with the Dao oneself ~ a living, shining exemplar of a life spent in Oneness with the Dao. Even though all are part of the same natural order, all individuals must harmonize with the Dao individually. For anyone attempting to harmonize and become one with the Dao, one of the best things that can happen to them is to run into another human being already in complete Oneness and harmony with the Dao. That would be a marvelous experience, and a wonderful catalyst to Daoist oneness.

What is Daoism's stance toward a utopia here on Earth? We have to remember that Daoism is primarily an individual activity, not a social one. However, to any individual Daoism offers the immediate experience of utopia ~ right here and right now ~ if the individual is in complete harmony and Oneness with the Dao. The individual's surrounding situation and/or environment is of no consequence. As long as the individual is in complete harmony and Oneness with the Dao, individuals will find themselves in the most perfect utopia. The individual will be "flowing with the flow," with joy and ecstasies and immortality following.

Given this Daoist approach to an earthly utopia, we have to surmise that the greater the number of individuals in harmony and Oneness with the Dao at any one moment, the more society will experience, overall, a social utopia.

There's promise here. For anyone looking to improve humanity's lot on this planet ~ and that's our goal, remember ~ Daoism may have something to offer to us in our pressing quest for an earthly utopia.

Together ~ thru the challenges of today ~

~ and into the promises of tomorrow

Expressions of Consciousness
2nd book of the *Bubbles of Consciousness* book series

Chapter 9 – Hinduism

Of the eleven expressions of collective human consciousness ~ or philosophies-of-life ~ that we have selected to
examine in this book, Hinduism is one of the oldest. Its tracea-
ble roots stretch way back ~ at least about 3,500 years back ~
to the prehistoric Iron Age of northwestern India, notably to
the ancient Vedic texts that were created sometime during that
period, as far as scholars can determine. Today Hinduism is the
third largest world religion, after Christianity and Islam respec-
tively, and has roughly one billion professed adherents. It is a
well-known expression of human conventional thinking.

Hinduism is mainly found on the Indian subcontinent,
with large numbers of followers also found in Bali, Nepal and
Bangladesh. Due to its prehistoric existence and continuous
development over thousands of years, Hinduism embraces an
extremely wide range of beliefs, and acknowledges an equally
wide range of authoritative sources, accumulated and accreted
over the many centuries. In fact, Hinduism is equally accepting
of such disparate concepts as (a) an unknowable transcendent
source of all existence, or (b) knowable personalized supreme
deities, or (3) atheism with its lack of belief in any type of su-

preme or transcendent entity. Tolerance of different beliefs ~ together with a far-reaching acceptance of the right to personal freedom in religious observance and practice ~ is a well-known hallmark of the Hindu belief system.

Despite the extremely wide range of beliefs found in Hinduism, most Hindus share three assumptive concepts, all three assumptive concepts being characteristic of the way that Hinduism is generally perceived both by its believers and by the rest of the world. In fact, many Hindus would agree that if an individual does not accept these three grounding assumptions without question, one would have to wonder if that person was truly a Hindu at heart.

Grounding Assumptions

The first common assumption in Hinduism is that all human beings possess a distinct, individual, eternal soul. Now ~ we have to be careful here. Usually ~ in most human belief systems ~ the concept of a *soul* implies the existence of a supreme or transcendent something that created that soul. In Hinduism, this is not necessarily the case. Some Hindus believe that the source of all existence is unknowable and unreachable. Some Hindus believe in a personalized god, or supreme being, or a number of supreme beings possibly being the various manifestations of the same transcendent entity. Some Hindus have no use for either of those two conceptualizations, arguing that the concept of an original, supreme being is not really necessary in dealing with human realities and arriving at human explanations.

Whatever the case, and whatever the individual standpoint, most Hindus accept the concept of a distinct individual, eternal soul regardless of their position as to where that soul might have come from in the first place.

The second common assumption in Hinduism is that these distinct, individual, eternal souls find themselves being continuously reborn into a succession of perishable, human bodies. A cycle of rebirth ~ or *reincarnation* ~ as it is generally thought of.

The soul puts on and takes off human bodies as a human being might change its clothes every day. While dwelling in, or wearing, these short-lived human bodies, the soul experiences pleasures ~ together with demarcating pains ~ although these pleasures are quite ephemeral, or transient, because experiencing these pleasures ceases at the moment of death, when the soul sheds the body.

The third common assumption in Hinduism is that the cycle of continuous rebirths is caused ~ or generated ~ by a mechanism or principle known as *karma*.

A clean and simple explanation of karma is that when the soul leaves a human body, if it has any unsatisfied desires or longings or things left unaccomplished, those unsatisfied desires cause the soul to reincarnate, or to be reborn, into a new human body. That way, the soul can have another chance at satisfying the unsatisfied desires left over from the previous lifetime. The unsatisfied longings cause the soul to want to return ~ over and over as long as the soul harbors any type of unsatisfied desires within itself.

Since, in ordinary human experience, the satisfaction of any one desire can and usually does engender a whole new grab bag of fresh desires ~ the ordinary soul always has a bunch of unsatisfied desires left over at the time of casting off the human body. Because of this, the karmic mechanism of rebirths is viewed as essentially endless.

Besides being viewed as the cause of endless rebirths, karma is also viewed as having another aspect, a quite important aspect. Karma acts as a sorting device, so to speak. Good deeds in a previous life can cause a good rebirth, whereas bad deeds in a previous life can cause a bad rebirth. Let's look at an illustrative example commonly offered in Hinduism.

Hindu society is customarily organized into a caste system. The four castes, in descending order, are (1) teachers and priests, (2) warriors, nobles and kings, (3) farmers, merchants and businesspeople, and (4) servants and laborers. Teachers and priests are considered the highest caste, while servants and laborers are considered the lowest caste ~ all on the same Hindu social ranking system. Now, suppose a soul did a bunch of good deeds while living as a servant or laborer ~ then that soul might be reborn as a farmer or a noble, or even better. Or suppose a soul did a bunch of bad deeds while living as a teacher or priest ~ then that soul might find itself coming back as a noble or a merchant, or even worse.

In this sense karma is considered both a causative mechanism of rebirths (unsatisfied desires at death), and an assessing determinant of what kind of rebirth a soul gets (how the previous life was lived). Depending on how a soul lives its various lives, it can go up and down the karmic ladder ~ repeatedly and endlessly.

So, there we have the three common and major grounding assumptions found in the Hindu belief system. First, the existence of distinct, individual, eternal souls. Second, a cycle of continuous rebirth of these souls into endless human lives yielding fleeting pleasures and pains. Third, a karmic mechanism that not only drives the rebirths, but also determines the nature of the next life that the soul is born into.

Sacred Goal

We shouldn't be surprised that in Hinduism the sacred goal is to escape from this cycle of endless rebirths with its transitory pleasures. The hope is that escape from karmic cycling will leave the soul in a place where pleasures are concrete and permanent ~ unending bliss ~ and not temporary and fleeting.

Achieving that sacred goal naturally breaks down into two goals, or "sub" goals, in a manner of speaking.

First, to permanently escape from the endless cycle of rebirths, one must break free from the "wheel" of karma. As long as a soul is stuck on the karmic wheel of rebirths, pleasures will come and go in a transitory fashion as the soul goes in and out of human bodies.

Second, one hopes that freedom from the endlessly spinning wheel of karma will leave one in a place where pleasure is permanent and eternal, often conceived as a blissful union with some sort of transcendent entity which is conceptualized as eternally in a state of limitless bliss, or unbroken pleasuring.

Those who conceive of ultimate reality as humanly unknowable may seek a unity with a supremely unknowable spirit. Those who conceive of ultimate reality as a personal deity may seek a unity with that particular deity. Those who do not bother to conceptualize an ultimate reality may seek a sense of Oneness with all the existing, living things that the individual is conscious of. The manner in which the individual conceptualizes ultimate reality will determine exactly what that individual will seek Oneness with ~ in order to get to that state of permanent and eternal pleasure.

In all cases, eternal bliss is seen as achievable by gaining a sense of ~ or a consciousness of ~ a pervasive Oneness and sameness assumed to be underlying all human realities, even if human existential appearances are deceiving. Therein lies the state of unbroken bliss ~ much better than transitory pleasures. Some sort of Oneness with a blissful something that is much greater than the individual self.

Of course, not all Hindu souls are equally ready to jump off the spinning wheel of karma. Some may be having more fun than others, and be perfectly willing to experience additional human lives. Those who are not quite ready to escape from the karmic wheel of rebirths will have goals other than immediate escape. They will mainly concentrate on three things during their human lives. One ~ living morally, or righteously, in order to improve the quality of the oncoming human lives. Two ~ building wealth to provide for human comforts during human existence. And three ~ experiencing sensual pleasures within a socially approved relationship, usually marriage. By pursuing these three goals in an appropriate manner it is hoped that when one is finally ready to jump off the spinning wheel of karma, the karmic load will be relatively light and jumping off will be relatively easy.

Other Hindu souls want to get off right now. They are tired of rebirth and want to achieve karmic escape in their current human life. For them the goal is simple and singular ~ karmic escape and the consequent attainment of endless bliss. For them wealth building and sensual pleasuring are unimportant. Their every effort during their life is bent to immediate karmic escape.

Path to the Sacred Goal

So ~ how does one escape from the karmic wheel of rebirths? A number of approaches or means are available, and the individual's selective practice of them will depend, of course, on how anxious the individual is to achieve karmic escape.

The study of sacred texts is always advisable, regardless of the individual's immediate goal regarding the revolving karmic wheel. The ancient Vedas and Upanishads are the oldest Vedic texts, with the *Rig Veda* probably being the oldest and most important one. In addition, Hindu epics such as the *Mahabharata* and *Ramayana* are also highly valued. The *Bhagavad Gita*, part of the *Mahabharata*, is an extremely popular text among the Hindus because it is viewed as a perfect exposition of the essential teachings of the Vedas and Upanishads. Then there are various puranas, sutras and tantras ~ all sacred texts that provide further instruction on how to minimize the effect of karma on a soul's wanderings thru various lifetimes.

Everyone endeavors to have lots of *dharma*, in Hinduism considered the moral and regulatory principle of the universe. A good life should be lived in tune with Dharma. Dharma not only minimizes karmic seeding, but also enhances the quality of the soul's next lifetime.

Good deeds engender dharma. One should speak only the truth, and if at all possible, keep it pleasant to hear. Non-violence is of utmost concern, together with compassion and sympathy for all living creatures. Opposing beliefs should be courteously and kindly tolerated. Stealing is forbidden, as are deceit and hypocrisy ~ only honesty, naturalness and sincerity are allowed. Self-control is highly prized, together with the charitable giving of oneself and one's possessions to others.

Of course, in the interest of maximizing dharma, bad deeds are to be avoided at all costs.

Now ~ as everyone knows ~ bad deeds are part and parcel of the human experience. But, even though a certain number of bad deeds may be unavoidable, they are to be minimized at all costs. A good Hindu way to offset the karmic effect of bad deeds and minimize the chance of continuing or repeating bad deeds is to develop self-control. Self-control can be developed thru such practices as austerities and mortifications, the study of sacred texts, fasting and celibacy, together with silence and meditation. The various yogas can be of tremendous help with self-control. Various religious deeds such as chanting, charity, pilgrimages, bathings and the observance of appropriate rituals can also offset the karmic effect of bad deeds.

There are four principal yogas, or strategies, for achieving the Hindu goals of karmic escape and endless bliss. *Bhakti* yoga emphasizes devotion to and love of deity as the best way to escape the karmic wheel and realize Oneness with eternal bliss. *Jnana* yoga emphasizes wisdom, or correct knowledge.

Karma yoga emphasizes correct action as the best way. *Raja* yoga emphasizes proper meditation.

Most Hindu commentators agree that these yogas are essentially inclusive of each other. For example, an individual pursuing bhakti yoga ~ emphasizing love of deity ~ will find that as devotion and love become perfected, so do wisdom, action, and meditation. Or, an individual pursuing karma yoga ~ emphasizing correct action as the way ~ will find that as action becomes perfected, so do love, wisdom and meditation. The yogas are not necessarily separate from each other, but rather differentiated in their emphasis on a particular strategy in pursuing karmic freedom and endless paradise.

Other practices are available to help Hindus maintain correct awareness thru-out the day, thereby maximizing dharma and minimizing the occurrence of bad deeds. Icons and images of heavenly beings and divine incarnations can be worshiped by lighting lamps and offering food, invocations, praise, and prayers in front of them. Chanting and the recitation of sacred texts during the day can keep the mind in correct awareness. Pilgrimages and bathings, especially during Hinduism's many religious festivals, can be of tremendous assistance. Personal devotion to divine avatars ~ considered incarnations of divinity in human forms ~ is widespread. Some of the more popular avatars are Vishnu, Brahma, Shiva, Shakti, Krishna, Durga, etc. In addition, following the teachings of gurus and Brahmin priests and providing sustenance to wandering holy ascetics such as sadhus and swamis will enhance the individual's dharma and minimize karma's effect.

Again, which practices are selected and the degree to which they are actually practiced is determined by the individual's position regarding the desirability of achieving karmic release quickly. For those who are not too anxious to jump off the karmic wheel of life, a comfortable progression thru Hinduism's four stages of life is perfectly acceptable ~ student, householder, retirement, and then asceticism.

During that progression, the appropriate practices will be observed together with pivotal life events ~ a baby's first partaking of food, the enrollment of children into formal education, an engagement to marry, and then eventual death. During all of that, the individual not too anxious to jump off the karmic wheel will be mainly concentrating on three things during their progression thru life ~ one, living morally, or righteously, in order to improve the quality of the oncoming human lives ~ two, building wealth to provide for human comforts during human existence ~ and, three, experiencing sensual pleasures within a socially approved relationship, usually marriage.

Others more anxious to get off the karmic wheel will skip all of that and head directly for asceticism. They will renounce the world together with its life stages of student, householder and retirement and enter into either a monastic or wandering existence of profound yogic practice and self-denial. Again, they will have no use for building material wealth or experiencing sensual pleasures. They want to get off the karmic wheel right now, and do not want to continue to experience rebirths together with its fleeting pleasures. They want permanent, eternal bliss ~ or endless pleasuring ~ quickly.

Stance Toward Earthly Utopia

Now that we have the gist of Hinduism somewhat laid out, let's see how we do with the rest of our research questions. So far, we have addressed grounding assumptions, sacred goals, and the avenues available to achieving those sacred goals.

What does Hinduism tell the individual about itself? Hinduism tells the individual that it is a distinct, individual, eternal soul captured in an endless cycle of rebirths that offer fleeting, transient pleasures. It tells the individual that as long as the individual has unfulfilled desires at death, it will be reborn again and again as a chance to satisfy those unsatisfied desires. It tells the individual that how it lives a previous life will determine what kind of life it gets the next time. And finally, it tells the individual that a good goal would be to find a way to get off this spinning wheel of human lifetimes and get to a place where pleasures are permanent and eternal, and not fleeting and transient. It tells the individual that all reality is grounded in a certain Oneness, and that realization of that Oneness is essentially the way to escape the cycle of rebirths. It offers to the individual a number of ways of accomplishing this.

Hinduism tells the individual that others are like it ~ captured in an endless cycle of rebirths that offer fleeting, transient pleasures. It tells the individual to be compassionate and tolerant of others, because there are many ways to achieve escape from rebirths with its fleeting pleasures. No one way is better than another, and they all lead to the same goal. There is no meaningful boundary between self and other, because all are on the same wheel of life and trying to get off it. All have the same goal of achieving unbroken happiness, or bliss. The only boundary that Hinduism offers to the individual per se is that of distinct, individual, eternal souls, and the relative progress that each is making in achieving escape from rebirths.

Hinduism doesn't talk to the desirability of achieving a social utopia here on Earth. Rather, it finds a personal utopia in the individual's permanently escaping from the human scene.

Because of that, Hinduism ~ despite its praiseworthy virtues of compassion, understanding, tolerance and nonviolence ~ is not necessarily a good candidate for those who wish to bring about a collective utopia right here on our planet ~ and bring it about quickly.

Together ~ thru the challenges of today ~
          ~ and into the promises of tomorrow

Expressions of Consciousness
2nd book of the *Bubbles of Consciousness* book series

Chapter 10 – Individualism

We have to be careful with this concept termed *individualism*. All human beings are subject to it; no one is exempt. Since the beginning of human time everybody has had some sort of individuality as part and parcel of their psyches. It's a simple matter of human physiology and the constraints of our biological existence. Let's take a look at natural ~ or innate ~ individuality before we examine modern individualism with its influential economic and political applications.

Innate Individualism

For all practical purposes, we are born alone, and we die alone. We come into this world all by ourselves, and we leave it all by ourselves. During that time, we each singularly possess a unique, individual physical body, and occupy it with a unique, individual consciousness that in turn experiences a unique, individual life flow. By ostensible physical laws, at any one time we each distinctly occupy a unique, individual point in time and space, with a unique point of perspective. Each of us is an individual ~ whether we like it or not. Each of us has a unique, individual perspective of existent reality, gained from our unique and individual existential conditions ~ consciousness, body delimitation, together with encompassing time and space. Individuality is engineered into the very structure of our awareness ~ we are all born into that.

Our innate individuality is driven by the determinants of human biology and physiology. Because of this, the innate elements of individuality will always be, in some manner or other, part of a person's inner being and resultant behavior ~ regardless of whatever mix of life-philosophies a person may be internalizing as a guide to feeling, thinking, living, and behaving. Something to keep in mind.

A succinct example of innate individualism can be found in the instinct for survival. The raw instinct for survival is found in individuals ~ not in groups. It's the individual that fights for biological life ~ not the group. A group, per se, doesn't have biology ~ a group is a collection of biologically distinct individuals. It's the individual that says, "I will live!" or "I will be!" This natural instinct for survival is one of the most fundamental forces driving the human individual, another being the drive to reproduce. It's hard wired into the individual's very being. Because of that, individuality and individualism are extremely strong forces in human affairs. They are ubiquitous, and no one can escape their influence. Any attempt to grapple with these fundamental forces ~ individuality and individualism ~ can be an exercise in frustration, unless one is very careful.

Of course, for purposes of our present analysis, we are concerned with individualism as it is currently found in the modern world we live in ~ that is, *modern individualism*. Today we find it as a pervasive "*ism*" ~ notably in the economic and political arenas. As a belief system and philosophy-of-life, modern individualism is a rather subtle but exceptionally powerful expression in today's collective human consciousness.

Modern Individualism

Modern individualism arose in Western Europe a handful of centuries ago as capitalism made its appearance in human affairs, both economically and politically. New philosophies of life were quickly needed to support and justify this new capitalistic development wherein ordinary individuals started amassing great material wealth for and to themselves. Modern individualism ~ with its assertion that the individual per se is of value in and of itself ~ quickly emerged as an important supporting philosophy.

Another supporting philosophy that gained great popularity during this time was the belief that great personal wealth signified ~ in the newly emergent Protestant faith ~ that the materially wealthy individual was perhaps favored by God and consequently also perhaps destined to go to the Protestant heaven instead of to the Protestant hell. Ancient Egyptians had parallel beliefs. We'll go into greater detail on histories in our next book. For our present purposes, let's go ahead and look at the grounding assumptions of modern individualism.

Grounding Assumptions

As we just noted, the grounding assumption in modern individualism is the idea that the individual ~per se ~ is of value in and of itself, and not just valued as a member of some group. In fact, individualism is essentially the opposite of collectivism, wherein it is the group that is viewed as of primary value. In collectivism, the needs of the group are viewed as far more important than the needs of any one individual. In modern individualism, it's the opposite ~ the needs of the individual are viewed as far more important than the needs of any group. In fact, in modern individualism, any group needs are considered as subordinate to and subject to the interests and needs of the individual.

The individual is considered to be its own "sovereign" ~ owing no natural allegiance to anyone or anything. The individual is considered to be rational and therefore capable of understanding itself and the world it finds itself in. Because of this, the individual is considered to be capable of managing its own affairs, and more importantly, its own survival. Consequently, in modern individualism, the individual is considered able to take care of itself without interference from anyone and anything ~ and has the unquestioned right to do so. Modern individualism expects each individual to look out for itself.

Relationships between individuals are kept situational and expedient. Relationships in a society dominated by modern individualism are much looser than in a society dominated by collectivism. Relationships are kept fluid because they are not an end in themselves ~ they are merely a temporary avenue for the pursuit of the individual's personal goals.

Sacred Goal

Given these grounding assumptions of modern individualism, the "sacred" goals are easy to ascertain ~ the maximization of the individual's happiness and the minimization of the individual's needs and wants. Everything else is secondary. It's all about the individual. The maximization of the individual's happiness and the minimization of the individual's needs and wants are primary, and the sole reason for existence ~ the *raison d'etre*.

Types of Modern Individualism

Let's take a moment to look at some of the more common, or well-known, manifestations of modern individualism in our world today. Modern individualism underpins today's dominant culture ~ known as "western culture" or "western civilization." It's primarily fueled by culture factories such as Hollywood ~ together with the capitalistic mass consumer marketing commonly associated with advertising centers such as Madison Avenue in New York. We'll look at three examples of different cultural expressions of modern individualism.

Libertinism is an expression of modern individualism that emphasizes the rather complete moral freedom of the individual. With a libertine person, raw hedonism comes to mind. The libertine seeks maximum pleasure, without thought for any consequence to others. Commitment to others is seen as having no value ~ an unnecessary restraint on the libertine's pursuit of personal pleasure. An example. A non-libertine might see value in keeping sexual behavior within a state of matrimony ~ sexual loyalty to a spouse. A libertine, on the other hand, might see value in sleeping with as many members of the other sex as possible ~ in order to maximize personal sexual pleasure

~ regardless of the consequences that may arise for the various sexual partners. Again, all for self ~ nothing for other.

Anarchism is an expression of modern individualism that emphasizes the right of the individual to participate only in voluntary organizations, and not be forced to participate in mandatory organizations. For example, strictly voluntary membership in a trade or labor organization would be okay. However, mandatory membership in governmental entities would not be okay. Even popular democracies meet with dis-approval from the anarchists. In the typical democracy, the majority in any geographical territory determine prevailing law, usually thru either direct or representative voting. However, those individuals who were not part of the successful voting, normally the minority, are still bound by what the majority vot-ed in. This is insufferable to an anarchist, because imposing majority rule on a minority violates the individual's right to only be bound by strictly voluntary associations and memberships. That is why anarchists are viewed as anti-government ~ only favoring "stateless" societies.

Liberalism is an expression of modern individualism that allows for mandatory membership in a state or government ~ but only a government that respects and protects the rights of the individual. That means that all individuals are respected and protected ~ not like in an absolute monarchy where the rights of only one individual are jealously guarded. This particular understanding is so fundamental in modern-day liberalism that in the United States it is written into the founding Declaration of Independence by reiterating John Locke's assertion that all individuals have the basic, natural right to pursue individual happiness, and that government primarily exists to guarantee and protect that right. In societies embracing liberalism, laws are passed ~ binding all ~ that allow individuals to pursue individual happiness by voluntarily associating with others thru voluntary contracts of mutual self-interest. This is what allows the existence of the many free markets in today's prevailing capitalist economies that are informed by modern liberalism. Contracts between individuals are indeed voluntary ~ but in turn are mediated by mandatory contract law.

Regardless of the particular expression of modern individualism that may be in play in the individual's life, just how does an individual go about pursuing maximum personal happiness? What does modern individualism ~ in general ~ say about the means or avenues appropriate to the pursuit?

Path to the Sacred Goal

There is a saying that all is fair in love and war. That is also true, in large part, in the pursuit of an individual's happiness in today's milieu of pervasive individualism. Everything goes, except perhaps breaking the law and getting punished. Even then, a sizeable number of individuals will knowingly break the law and risk the resulting punishment because they feel that it is worth it in pursuit of their ultimate prize ~ their personal happiness. That, of course, is where liberalism takes on overtones of libertinism.

From the individual's perspective, everything in the surrounding environment is subject to being bent to the will of the individual, and utilized to maximize the individual's personal happiness. Any sense of ethics or morality is expedient and strictly situational, with individuals using the psychological strategy of rationalization to minimize embarrassment or shame within their own psyche. Relationships are kept practical and mostly temporary, again with inner rationalization maintaining a sense of personal rightness. The relatively loose sexual standards and high divorce rates observed in western societies can be seen as an illuminating example of how the concept of individualism plays out in today's modern societies.

Again ~ as to the means available to the individual in pursuing personal happiness ~ everything goes as long as one can safely get away with it. Corruption becomes pervasive.

Modern individualism tells the individual that it is a god unto itself, answering to none other ~ the center of its own universe. It tells the individual that it is capable of managing its own affairs, and should not countenance any unwanted interference. It tells the individual that the only moral precept or ethic that it should observe is the unbridled pursuit of its own personal happiness. Everything that the individual is conscious of should be harnessed to that end. Today's well-known advertising jingle ~ be all that you can be ~ is an eloquent testimony to that dictum.

Modern individualism tells the individual that other human beings are merely environmental objects to be manipulated and bent to the self's will. Much of this happens via negotiated contracts of mutual self-interest. However, today we still have far, far more aggressive manipulations of other human beings taking place. Human trafficking in child labor and the sex trade is still a widespread global phenomenon, as is slavery for menial labor. And all of this is driven by some individual's pursuit of their own personal happiness.

The boundary between self and other is absolute. Self is sovereign; other is manipulated. Other is fodder for the needs and wants of the self. The only conceivable way that the boundary between self and other might be breached is thru strong emotional attachments such as love. In human affairs, love seems to be a dissolving solvent that can breach the boundary between individuals and meld self and other into an empathic whole. It can cause the individual to view the happiness of another as equally important as its own happiness ~ perhaps even more so. Outside of that, the individualistic self only sees others as numerous pawns on the chessboard of personal happiness.

Stance Toward Earthly Utopia

Individualism does not offer us much in the way of utopia. Any utopia it may have to offer is intended for the individual ~ not for the group. We, of course, are looking for a social utopia, and a quick one at that.

However, given the innate strength and ubiquity of human individuality, we do know that we will have to directly address human individuality when conceiving our new social utopia. Any attempt to sidestep or ignore it will doom us to failure. After all, we are all individuals, and our social utopia will be made up of individuals, each and all quite taken with their own unique and personal individualities. In human affairs, human individuality cannot be ignored.

Perhaps we can find a way to positively and productively use human individuality as one of our building blocks in bringing about our much sought after new social utopia.

Chapter 11 – Islamism

Being the world's second largest religion on the planet ~ after Christianity ~ and easily responsible for generating lots of newsworthy events around the globe, Islamism is a philosophy of life worthy of our investigation. As conventional thinking goes, it is the third monotheistic religion to spring from the Abrahamic stream of writings, or books ~ the other two religions being Judaism and Christianity. As a major expression of collective human consciousness, it is found all over the world, with large numbers on the Asian and African continents.

An Islamic adherent ~ known as a *Muslim* ~ usually belongs to one of three well-known Islamic subgroups ~ *Sunni, Shia* or *Sufi*. The term *Islam* means peace or submission to God, known as *Allah* in Islam. For a Muslim, the term *Allah* means "the one true god." Visually, the Islamic influence is rather easy to spot. All over the world, Islam's sacred places of worship ~ known as mosques ~ are singularly devoid of any images, carvings or depictions of living beings or things, but rather covered by inscriptions of quotes from its most sacred text, the *Koran* ~ or *Qur'an*.

Let's look at Islam's grounding assumptions. There are a number of them ~ all equally important to a devout Muslim.

Grounding Assumptions

Islam's first group of grounding assumptions has to do with the nature of Allah. Allah is the one supreme being ~ transcendent and never assuming human form. Allah is omnipotent, just, and merciful. Being omnipotent, Allah's will is supreme, and everything that occurs is predestined according to Allah's supreme, omnipotent will. In the course of Creation, Allah has given human beings the free will to choose between right action (good) or wrong action (evil) as they make their way thru their human lives amid Allah's myriad predestined events, or happenings.

Islam's second group of grounding assumptions has to do with the purpose of the human being. In Islamism, a human being's purpose is to submit to, serve, and worship Allah. And, everyone only has one human life to do that. After that, it is bodily resurrection in the afterlife to face the Day of Judgment ~ the sorting out of the good from the wicked. Good Muslims (and good Jews and good Christians ~ peoples of "the book") get to go to Heaven, while Hell is reserved for bad Muslims (and bad Jews and bad Christians) and nonbelievers of "the book" ~ the Abrahamic stream of writings.

Islam's third group of grounding assumptions has to do with the help or guidance that Allah provides to humans so that they can make good choices in their lives instead of bad choices. Muslims believe that Allah's help and guidance come in three major forms.

First, there are the sayings of the Islamic prophet Muhammad, the last and final true prophet in a succession of prophets of "the book" ~ "the book" substantially being the biblical Old Testament, then the biblical New Testament, and finally the Koran containing Muhammad's divine revelations. Muslims believe that Islam is an eternal religion existing from the dawn of Creation. In that view, the major prophets preceding Muhammad are notably Abraham, Moses, Elijah, and Jesus. Prophets are assumed to appear periodically to clarify the divine message to humanity, since the last prophet's sayings may have gotten confused and misinterpreted with the passage of time. For Muslims, Muhammad is the last and final true prophet sent by Allah to humanity, and the Koran is the final word of Allah.

Second, there is the way that the prophet Muhammad lived his life. To the highest degree possible, life as Muhammad lived it is to be emulated by every Islamic adherent. His life was well documented by those around him, so questions about how Muhammad did things or how he handled issues can be readily determined from historic documentaries. Any question or issue becomes "what would the Prophet Muhammad have done?"

Finally, Muslims firmly believe in the existence of angels. Angels were created by Allah to help humans find the right way and make the right choices during their lives. Angels are viewed as the messengers of Allah, with no free will of their own ~ they embody and express only the will of Allah. Angels communicate divine revelations, such as the Koranic revelations given to Muhammad by the angel Gabriel. They also record a person's actions during life, and then collect the soul upon death. Since Allah is strictly transcendent and does not take on form, angels perform this function instead. This is why angels are deemed so sacred and important in Islamism.

All of the above are the grounding assumptions that are accepted without question by all Islamic believers, or Muslims.

Sacred Goal

The sacred goal for a Muslim is obvious ~ to conduct oneself during one's life so that upon bodily resurrection at the Day of Judgment one gets sent to Heaven instead of to Hell.

Path to the Sacred Goal

Of course, in Islam, the way to get to Heaven is to practice total submission to Allah during one's lifetime through appropriate worship and action. Since Islamism permeates every single facet of a Muslim's life ~ whether private or public ~ there are a lot of things that a Muslim must do to have a good chance of ending up in Heaven on the Day of Judgment. Let's start with the extremely important *Pillars of Islam*.

The Pillars of Islam are five mandatory acts that all faithful Muslims must perform during their lives. Exceptions do not come easily. Since the five Pillars are so important, let's review them one at a time.

First, each and every Muslim must recite the foundational creed that goes something like this ~ *"there is no god but Allah, and Muhammad is the messenger of God."* This recitation must be done under oath and in front of witnesses, and always during prayer. The more a Muslim recites this creed, the better. This recital is the most fundamental testimony of faith in Islam.

Second, each and every Muslim must ritually pray to Allah a minimum of five times a day, preferably at a mosque. Prayers must always contain the recital of the fundamental testimony of faith, together with other recitals from the Koran. During these prayers, Muslims prostrate themselves in the direction of the Kaaba in Mecca. Mecca is the holiest city in Islam, and the Kaaba is the holiest shrine in the Islamic world. It was in Mecca that Islamism started, and it was at the Kaaba that Muhammad first took a hard stand for his new faith. To make sure that no one inadvertently overlooks or forgets the critical prayer times, mosques all around the world loudly call out to the faithful to come together to pray ~ again, at least five times a day.

Third, each and every Muslim must give alms to the poor, the heartbroken, the needy, the stranded, etc. This duty is not seen as voluntary, but rather as a mandatory religious requirement. Required minimums are set, but Muslims are encouraged to give even more than the required minimums as an act of voluntary charity and good faith.

Fourth, each and every Muslim must fast during the daylight hours during the month of *Ramadhan* ~ the month during which Muhammad started receiving his divine revelations. Some exceptions are allowed, such as medical needs. However, if allowed exceptions are used, the fasting requirement is expected to be made up as soon as possible. Fasting during the night hours is not expected, nor required.

Fifth, each and every Muslim must make a pilgrimage ~ *Hajj* or *Umrah* ~ to Mecca at least once during one'' lifetime. The designated time for the all-important Hajj pilgrimage is during *Dhu-al-Hijjah* ~ the last month of the Islamic calendar. The Umrah pilgrimage can be carried out any time during the year. Some things accomplished during a pilgrimage would be walking around the Kaaba seven times, retracing the steps of historical figures important to Islamism, and praying in the desert at historically sacred spots. Exceptions are available if the reason is pressing, such as physical disability or exceptional difficulty in negotiating distances, or financial hardship.

So, these are the five Pillars of Islam ~ proper recital and testimony, prayer at least five times a day, continuous almsgiving and charity, fasting for a month each year, and at least one pilgrimage to Mecca during one's lifetime. Dutiful observance of these five Pillars is a major step toward Heaven on the Day of bodily resurrection and Judgment.

There are a number of other things a Muslim is expected to do in order to have a respectable showing on the Day of Judgment. Let's look at some of them.

In Islam, the use of alcohol is banned, as are illegal drugs, the consumption of pork, and gambling. The hoarding of wealth is not allowed ~ that's where continuous alms giving comes in. Instead of hoarding, wealth should be responsibly lent out, but not with usurious interest rates. On a daily basis, a faithful Moslem should concentrate on maximizing good deeds and minimizing bad deeds. Around the onset of puberty, a Muslim starts being held accountable for personal behavior. Bad deeds can be offset through appropriate repentance and a host of subsequent good deeds.

A good Muslim respects and upholds Islamic law. Remember, in Islam, there is no separation of religion and government. Islamic societies are not secular societies, in which religion and government are kept distant at arm's length. In Islamic societies, sacred texts dictate law and policy, the foremost text being the Koran. If further resource is needed, then the life of Muhammad is examined to see how the Prophet would have handled a similar question. After that, the Abrahamic stream of writings is utilized including the Old Testament and the New Testament together with other ancient, respected scrolls. If all of the foregoing still do not avail, then as a last resort the consensus of Islamic jurists together with analogical reasoning would probably be employed to assist in achieving an Islamic resolution of the issue at hand.

A good Muslim observes the Islamic holidays. The *Eid Al-Fitr* holiday is celebrated when yearly month-long fasting ends on the last day of Ramadan. The giving of gifts together with gatherings of family and friends is typical of appropriate celebrations for the Eid Al-Fitr. Another important holiday in the Islamic calendar is *Eid al-Adha* ~ celebrating the utmost importance of submitting to the will of Allah. It commemorates the Biblical story of Abraham's readiness and willingness to sacrifice his only son if Allah so commanded it. Acts of charity together with sacrifices of animals are usually employed as appropriate celebrations for the Eid al-Adha holiday.

A good Muslim will be a married Muslim. Islam is a religion that encourages neither celibacy nor monasticism nor asceticism. On the contrary, marriage is encouraged with each husband having up to four lawful wives, together with the commensurate children. The husband is the head of the household, with wives recognizing this by wearing veils in public and otherwise remaining relatively secluded within the family. A Muslim that does not marry and enter into the family way would be viewed as not meeting the expectations of Islamism.

As a final means of reaching the sacred goal ~ assignment to Heaven instead of to Hell on the Day of Judgment ~ a good Muslim will constantly practice what is known as *jihad*. Often interpreted as violent warfare by western societies and extremist Muslims, jihad actually suggests a peaceful struggle ~ against anything that doesn't meet Islamic standards. Frequently misconstrued in meaning, a jihad strongly implies an internal struggle, as the individual attempts to root out any personal thought and behavior that are not approved in Islamism. A constant jihad within the individual is an excellent way to be a dutiful Moslem. Properly understood, jihad should be viewed as a rather peaceful activism for Islam, especially within oneself.

So, what is Islam's stance toward the individual? What does Islam tell the individual about itself?

Islamism tells the individual that it was created to ~ and exists solely to ~ serve and worship Allah, via total submission to Allah's omnipotent will. Allah's will can be found in the Koran, containing the Prophet Muhammad's divine revelations. If the individual performs well during life, after death it will go to Heaven. If not, then it's off to Hell. It's an antipodal choice, with no in-between or alternatives. And, the individual has only one lifetime to measure up to Allah's expectations as outlined in Islam's sacred texts.

What is Islam's stance toward other? What does Islam tell the individual about other human beings?

Islamism doesn't tolerate racial prejudice or religious bigotry. It teaches that all people are equally considered the children of Adam, biblically the first human being. It also teaches that all children are born pure, and that it is parental teaching that directs a child to a particular religion. An attitude of peace, together with mercy and forgiveness, is the proper attitude toward another human being. Muslims are not expected to aggressively proselytize Islamism, but rather peacefully and gently share the teachings with non-believers. Then, it is up to the non-believer to act upon the sharing, one way or the other.

If there is a boundary between self and other, it would be between believers and nonbelievers. Or, it would be between people of "the book" and people "not" of the book. The boundary can be breached through a sincere conversion to Islamism, unless one is already a sincere Jew or Christian.

Stance Toward Earthly Utopia

In Islamism, any sense of utopia is reserved for the afterlife, in the form of an assignment to Heaven for those who are found to have lived a good live while on earth. For Muslims, utopia on earth today is not a workable idea. Life on earth is viewed more as a time of personal trial and testing of the individual's sincere submission to Allah's will ~ a prelude to what awaits the individual upon the Day of Judgment.

Despite its profound message of peace and goodwill to each and all, anyone looking for a utopia right here and right now on Earth might not find useful support in Islamism. For the Muslim, any chance of utopia is strictly on the other side of death.

Chapter 12 – Judaism

One of the oldest world religions being practiced today, Judaism is the foundational belief system for two other philosophies-of-lives that developed centuries after Judaism itself ~ namely, Christianity and Islamism. Both offshoots of Judaism, Christianity and Islamism happen to be the two largest religions on our planet right now ~ in terms of professed adherents.

As an expression of conventional human consciousness, Judaism's actual adherents number less than one percent of the global population. They are mostly found in Israel and North America, with smaller populations located in other countries and in other areas. However, despite its extremely small population size relative to other major expressions of conventional human consciousness, Judaism has had a hugely disproportionate influence upon the legal systems, ethical standards and religious assumptions in many other societies and civilizations, mostly western ones.

Today, Judaism is diversely practiced by subgroups such as orthodox, conservative, reform, reconstructionist, humanistic, etc. ~ each with its own view as to exactly what Judaism is, and how it is to be properly observed and practiced. Regardless of what may be the exact approach in any particular subgroup ~ the various Jewish communities scattered around the globe, generally speaking, tend to be led by scholarly rabbinical authorities. In turn, these rabbinical authorities are guided by a host of ancient and sacred texts. Obviously, given Judaism's history spanning more than 3,000 years, a number of different ways have evolved to observe and practice it. So, we will have to be careful to characterize this philosophy-of-life by the most common ways that most Jewish adherents observe and practice today.

Grounding Assumptions

Let's first look at Judaism's ancient, grounding assumptions. They are said to stretch all the way back to the Iron Age in the Middle East ~ roughly three to four thousand years ago.

Judaism is a monotheistic religion. Its first and foremost assumption forms the very backbone of its ancient belief system ~ there is only one God, and that one God is both transcendent and immanent. There are no other gods. Graven images of that which is both transcendent and immanent are impossible. There is just one and only one God. And, this one

God is ~ simultaneously ~ both vastly superior to existence as we know it (transcendent), and yet fundamentally intrinsic in every aspect of that very same existence that we know and experience every moment and every day (immanent).

Judaism's second grounding assumption is that humanity is created in the divine image. Many Jews believe that each individual has a singular and private relationship with God, and that each individual's relationship with God is equally important in the overall scheme of things. No one person is better than another. God has given to individuals the tremendous potential to act, together with the free will to make free choices. Individuals are responsible to both God and their fellow humans for how they act and what they do, the choices they choose to make, and the consequences that follow from their acts and from their choices.

Judaism's third grounding assumption is that the Jewish people have a special relationship with God ~ namely ~ that the Jewish people have somehow been uniquely chosen by God to guide general humanity into holiness through God's commandments together with Jewish teachings and examples. For the purposes of holiness, what an individual does is considered to be far more important than how an individual thinks.

God has laid down ten major commandments to guide human behavior, together with numerous minor commandments.

In return for accepting this unique role in guiding humanity into holiness, Jews believe that God has given them a covenant to the effect that the Jewish people have an exclusive claim on lands at the eastern end of the Mediterranean Sea, and that the Jewish people will greatly multiply on Earth. Circumcision of Jewish males is the mark and sign recognizing this age-old Covenant with the Jewish God. All this is documented in the *Torah* ~ the five ancient books written by Moses, acknowledged by Jews to be their greatest prophet.

Many Jews also believe that another Jewish prophet will arise sometime in the future ~ a Messiah, so to speak. This Jewish Messiah is expected to usher in a period of peace and goodwill on Earth, and permanently establish the Jewish people as a divinely ordained ruling kingdom in their promised lands ~ the lands promised to them by God via the Covenant.

Sacred Goal

The sacred goal in Judaism is self-evident ~ namely, to keep the Covenant alive for its promises, and to have a good placing in any possible afterlife and the Messiah's new kingdom whenever it might arrive. To do this, of course, the Jews have to conduct themselves in such a way that the way they live and act are recognizable as obvious lives of holiness, and fit examples for general humanity to follow on the path to holiness.

The key to that, in turn, is to obey the commandments. Obeying the commandments is the means to get to the sacred goal. Remember, in Judaism the emphasis is on acts, not thoughts. Obeying the commandments as one goes thru the day is the Judaic key to holiness. There's lots of commandments to observe ~ not only the ten major ones, but also lots of secondary commandments. Let's go over some of the things that Jews do on a daily basis in order to maintain the promises of their Covenant with their God.

Path to the Sacred Goal

The *Torah* ~ Moses' five books ~ underlies everything that Jews do. It contains all the commandments that must be observed and followed in every aspect of Jewish life. The *Torah* is the basis not only of the law of the land, but also of how a daily life is to be lived from moment to moment. In addition to the ten major commandments, there are more than six hundred minor commandments to heed. A large number of the six hundred minor commandments are considered impractical to follow in a modern era, but the ten major commandments allow no deviance, even in today's world. These commandments are generally codified into formal law in a number of modern-day countries ~ so let's quickly review them in turn.

The "*I am*" is the God of humanity, and the "*I am*" is the only God that exists. (2) No graven images or idols of God shall be fashioned or worshiped in any form. (3) The name of God shall be considered sacred, and not used profanely. (4) One day a week shall be considered to be more Holy than the other six days of the week; this day shall be known as the Sabbath and observed as a day of rest from the mundane chores and duties of daily living. (5) Children shall honor their parents. (6) The killing or murder of another human being is forbidden. (7) Adultery is forbidden. (8) Stealing is forbidden. (9) Lying is forbidden, especially about others. (10) Wanting something that belongs to another is also forbidden, especially another person's spouse. These are the ten commandments that are generally observed and codified as law in so many countries and societies today.

If an individual should have questions about the various commandments as they are found in the *Torah*, numerous commentaries exist that may be of assistance. These commentaries were developed over thousands of years as the Jews encountered a wide variety of living conditions and hardships that caused confusion as to how Judaism was to be observed and practiced during difficult times. Some of the more well-known commentaries popularly used today are the *Midrash*, the *Talmud*, and the *Mishnah*. There are many more commentaries available that are variously used by the diverse subgroups found within Judaism. If the commentaries don't completely help, then recourse can be had to a *rabbi*. A rabbi is a recognized scholar learned and well versed in the *Torah* together with any applicable commentaries that may bear on the question at hand.

The *Torah* is considered so important in Judaism that it must be studied constantly and each year fully read in its entirety. In fact, the daily reading and study of the *Torah* is considered an act of Holiness within itself. However, given so many commandments to follow and observe, many Jews needed a quick core summary of the essential Jewish beliefs. That summary was provided by a Jewish rabbinic scholar during the Middle Ages, and is known as Maimonides' (Moshe ben Maimon) thirteen required aspects of Jewish belief.

The *13 Principles of Faith* cover such things as the nature of God, the position of Moses within the Jewish community, and the importance of the *Torah* to anyone professing to be a Jew. The reward of good-doers and the punishment of evildoers is acknowledged and accepted, as is the expectation of a Jewish Messiah in the future. At the time of the coming of the Jewish Messiah, the resurrection of the dead is assumed, together with final judgment. All this is declared in the *13 Principles of Faith* and professed by most Jews.

Since Judaism is a philosophy-of-life that concentrates on actual acts instead of just inner beliefs, it is thought of as an ethical religion, or an ethical belief system. Jews are expected to act morally at all times. Qualities of character that come to mind would be truthfulness, justness, humbleness, mercifulness, goodwill and respect for oneself and others. Unnecessary negative speech should be avoided and replaced with charity of will and deed. Through constant ethical behavior, Jews effectively take care of humanity and God's Creation by always doing the correct and right thing in accordance with the commandments contained within the *Torah*. Unremitting ethical behavior is considered the way to be holy within the expectations of the Covenant.

A quick way to think on one's feet as to the appropriate behavior at any moment or in any situation is to truly love both God and one's fellow human being ~ and to act out that love instead of keeping it inside to oneself.

In Judaism, thinking holiness is not enough. It must be acted out and made visible.

Jews are expected to pray to their God at least three to four times a day. A key prayer is the recitation and remembrance of the first commandment ~ *Hear, O Israel! The Lord is our God! The Lord is One!* Frequent prayer is a way to help remember the exacting requirements of Judaism, even when a busy day may get even more hectic.

Holidays are important. Observing the Sabbath every week is by far the most important holiday, since it is the subject of one of the ten major commandments. Other important holidays are observed yearly. Let's look at a few of the more well-known ones.

Every year Jews observe a ten-day period during which they make amends for any bad deeds that they may have committed during the preceding year. *Rosh Hashanah*, the Jewish New Year, marks the beginning of this ten-day period. During the ten-day period, not only are Jews expected to make amends and otherwise repent for bad deeds, but they are also expected to sincerely attempt to mend any injured relationships wherein they may have offended another. The end of the ten-day period is marked by *Yom Kippur*, considered the holiest annual day in the Jewish calendar. It marks the end of the ten-day formal period of atonement, and is celebrated with community fasting, prayer, and celebration.

More recently the holiday known as the Festival of Lights ~ *Hanukkah* ~ has become increasingly popular. Hanukkah lasts about eight days, and happens to occur around the same time as the Christmas holidays observed by Christians. It formally commemorates a miracle said to have occurred during a rededication of the ancient Jewish Temple in Jerusalem centuries ago. The miracle concerns an eternal flame that had to be kept burning continuously in the Temple. The oil feeding the lamp only had one day's supply left, but the flame burned for seven additional days ~ without any apparent oil ~ until it was possible to replenish the oil in the usual way. During Hanukkah, lights are lit each night in remembrance of the miracle of the Light in the Jewish Temple so long ago.

Other holidays are important to pious Jews. The *Passover* holiday commemorates the delivery of the Jews from lives of bondage and slavery in ancient Egypt. The *Tabernacles* holiday commemorates the wandering of the Jews for forty years in the wilderness just after their delivery from Egypt, but before they arrived at the lands promised in the Covenant. The *Pentecost* holiday commemorates the gift of the *Torah* to Moses and the Jewish people during their forty years of wandering in the wilderness. These three events are recorded as historical occurrences in the *Torah*.

Since the ancient Jewish Temple in Jerusalem no longer exists, Jewish communities hold services and pray together in houses of worship generally known as *synagogues*. The architectural design of synagogues varies widely, but inside are normally found certain common items. Scrolls of the *Torah* are kept in a sheltered place, referred to as an ark. A place is reserved in front of the ark for praying. A reader's space, usually elevated, is provided for the reading of the *Torah* and the direction of the communal worship. Lastly, just as in the ancient Temple in Jerusalem, a light is continually lit in remembrance of ancient Temple times.

Judaism is well known for its *kosher* rules, and kosher foods are highly respected all around the world. These kosher rules are found in the many commandments contained in the *Torah*. Kosher rules touch on things like what kind of animals can be eaten, and how they must be slaughtered and prepared. As an example, pork is forbidden. Slaughter must be quick and relatively painless. Kosher rules even touch on the utensils used in handling kosher foods, whether serving utensils or preparation utensils. The preparation of alcoholic products is also subject to kosher rules. For Jews, observance of kosher rules is a religious exercise in holiness by staying within the dictates of the Covenant. Conversely, for much of the world population that holds kosher foods in such a high regard, it is an appreciation of the high level of hygiene that is generally associated with kosher preparation.

Jews are also known for wearing a skull cap, otherwise known as a yarmulke or *kippa*. It's round, and can cover either the whole skull, or part of it. The kippa is usually brimless, and made of different materials and in various designs. Its religious significance is twofold. First, wearing it is considered an act of humility by keeping one's head covered in the omnipresence of God. Second, it's a reminder, by being placed on the top of the head, that there is something far greater in Creation than the ordinary intellect of a human being ~ there is a Transcendent God to be acknowledged and obeyed unceasingly.

The *bar mitzvah* is an extremely important and relatively well-known Jewish celebration. It is the formal rite of passage from childhood into adulthood. It occurs around the age of twelve or thirteen, and happens for both males and females. Celebration of the arrival into adulthood is usually commemorated by having the new young adult perform an important adult task, such as leading a community in worship and publicly reading from the *Torah*. The life events of birth, marriage and death also have their respective celebrations. The important rite of circumcision of male children is usually associated with the birth event.

The *Star of David* is well known as the popular symbol of Judaism. It's a six-pointed star, made by superimposing an equilateral triangle on top of an identical equilateral triangle at 180 degrees. It is conceptually thought of as symbolic of the "shield" or protection of David, Judaism's most famous king from ancient times. It is from King David's genetic line that the future Messiah is supposed to come ~ as another "shield" for the Jewish community and for holiness at large. In some Jewish texts, the concept "Shield of David" goes further than just thinking of David and his offspring as protectors of the Jews. These texts suggest thinking of God as the shield of David during David's own hard times, as recorded in the ancient history books of the Jews ~ and also suggest thinking of God as the shield of all holy and observant Jews.

A review of the most common aspects of Judaism today is incomplete without mentioning the *Western Wall* in Jerusalem. The Western Wall is all that's left of the ancient Temple complex in ancient Jerusalem. Jews pilgrimage to it every day to pray to their God and weep over what happened to the Jewish people two thousand years ago ~ that's why it is famously known as the *Wailing Wall.* Today it is perhaps the most sacred site in Judaism, and a potent reminder of Judaism's turbulent history.

The foregoing gives us a thumbnail sketch of Judaism as it is generally observed and practiced today.

Stance Toward Earthly Utopia

How does Judaism speak to our research questions? How does it talk to the individual and to the concept of a global utopia? Let' see.

Judaism tells an individual Jew that it is part of a special group of people, primarily defined through ancient bloodlines. That is, a Jew is told that it is part of an age-old kinship group ~ a large family spread around the globe numbering about ten million or more people ~ with common ancestors going back thousands of years. It is told that as a member of this very old kinship group it enjoys a special relationship with the Jewish God. That relationship is laid out in the unique Covenant that the Jewish people feel that they have with their God. The individual Jew is told that as a member of the Jewish community, it is expected to do its part in observing the numerous requirements of the Covenant, so that all Jews can receive and enjoy the important promises contained in their Covenant.

Consequently, Judaism tells the individual Jew that non-Jews are outsiders ~ that is, not chosen to have that special Covenant relationship with God. However, in keeping with the Covenant mandate to the effect that all Jews manifest holy behavior at all times and toward all peoples, the individual Jew is expected to treat non-Jews fairly and lovingly ~ as the Jew would want to be treated itself ~ the proverbial Golden Rule.

Because of the bloodline delimitations, the boundary between Jew and non-Jew is somewhat hard and fast. Judaism does not encourage conversion to Judaism by non-Jews, primarily because of the kinship protocols. To be specific, Judaism does not *dis*-courage conversion; it merely does not *en*-courage it. However, if a non-Jew is sincerely determined to become a Jew through and through ~ accepting the teachings and obligations contained within the *Torah* together with its many commentaries ~ then that person is fully accepted and welcomed into the Jewish community as a Jew.

As we noted earlier, Judaism is a philosophy-of-life that focuses far more on the here-and-now than on possible afterlives. Not only do the tenets of Judaism focus on the here and now, but they also focus far more on acts performed than on ideas thought. Judaism wants humanity *acting* holy in our present lives here on Earth.

Expressions of Consciousness
2nd book of the *Bubbles of Consciousness* book series

That makes Judaism one of the expressions of conventional human consciousness that seeks a utopia in the present, and not in the distant future in some sort of afterlife. And, that orientation to the present makes Judaism a compelling candidate to help us in our quest for a quick utopia as a fix to our current problems. We too ~ we want our new utopia right here and right now.

Chapter 13 – Science

If there is a prevailing form of collective human consciousness today, it would have to be that which we term *modern science*. Modern science is a predominant conventional thinking of the day all over our planet. As an intensely practiced philosophy-of-life it has dramatically changed the way humans had thought and lived for the thousands of years before modern science made its appearance about five to six centuries ago. It has brought countless benefits to humanity. However, these countless benefits appear to have come hand-in-hand with unanticipated and rather stygian costs.

Before modern science made its appearance on the global stage, life for humanity was generally short-lived and physically hard. Everything had to be produced by individual, backbreaking toil. Need some food? Plant and harvest it yourself using only hand tools and beasts of burden. Need clothes? Gather the raw material, spin the thread, and then weave the material and cut a garment out of it ~ all by hand. Need to go somewhere? Either walk or ride a donkey. Need a sip of water? Draw it up out of the well with a bucket. Need to communicate with someone at a distance? Start walking.

Every need had to be met with personal, physical effort. Because of that, human bodies wore out relatively quickly, and life was generally short with many people dying in their thirties or forties, simply out of the exhaustion of living the daily life and coping with its unremitting physical demands.

Advantages

Today, modern science's technologically savvy products reduce most of that backbreaking labor for us. Now, it's a push-button world. In addition, modern science has given us new medical technology that has pushed back many age-old diseases and plagues. Newborns and children have generally stopped dying in their early years and now grow up to live useful and enjoyable lives. At the present time, with the technological advancements of modern science, many of us easily live into our eighties and nineties. All because modern science has given us tools that reduce most backbreaking physical labor ~ and equally importantly ~ also because modern science has stamped down the old life-threatening diseases and plagues of yesteryear.

Obviously, this is cause for great rejoicing. We live much longer, and don't have to break our backs doing it. However, before we get too happy, we had better look at the disturbing side consequences of modern science. There are two consequences in particular that we need to consider.

Disadvantages

The first consequence that we need to consider is modern science's direct impact on our environment.

Scientific discoveries have indeed led to many new technologically advanced and wondrous products, but the production of these wondrous new products has spawned numerous toxic side effects ~ generally contaminating the pristine environment that we enjoyed before modern science made its appearance. Cancers are now a way-of-life for many ~ plausibly exacerbated by these new man-made toxins continuously being dumped into our environment. Autism is on an alarming rise ~ babies are being malformed in the womb, again plausibly caused by the new toxins. Pervasive drug use is causing human intelligence to decline. Many species are becoming extinct, deprived of their normally uncontaminated, pristine environment. The atmospheric ozone layer is weakening, allowing harmful cosmic radiation to threaten all biological life on Earth.

A direct result of modern science's marvelous new products is that our otherwise unsullied environment has become a veritable cesspool of manufactured poisonous toxins ~ and it is destroying life as we know it, including our own species.

The second consequence that we need to consider is a direct result of the first consequence.

When modern science gave us increased longevity and the ability to live relatively free from age-old diseases, the human population exploded. Many, many more humans survived childbirth and childhood, and went on to live much longer lives than earlier generations. Of course, this explosion in the human population meant an explosion in the consumer population, and this in turn demanded the increasing mass production of modern science's new marvels. And ~ of course ~ that in turn meant the accelerated dumping of poisonous toxins into the environment, together with attendant global warming.

Global warming further exacerbates the environmental issues. We are facing increasingly violent weather, the release of toxins locked for ages in permafrost, and changes in ocean chemistry and dynamics, such as acidification of the oceans and changes in the flows of the primary ocean currents. Our precious planet might be able to sustain a population of about three billion human beings, yet the current population is more than twice that and still climbing. This chain of population dynamics has resulted in resource exhaustion, species extinction, and multifarious pollution ~ all over the globe.

Equally alarming, the advances that early modern science had brought to humanity in controlling the age-old diseases and plagues are now being quickly eroded by the appearance of increasingly drug-resistant super-pathogens.

Obviously modern science comes to us with both blessings and cursings, and we seem to be irresistibly caught within that dangerously conflicted grip. This grave position that modern science has humanity trapped into is so threatening to our continued existence that we must very carefully examine the foundations of the edifice that modern science has built for us. It's now time to look at what modern science is all about, particularly its grounding ~ or unquestioned assumptions. That's right! As a philosophy of life modern science is not exempt ~ it too has grounding assumptions that must be accepted "without question" by its followers.

However, before we get into the grounding assumptions, let's look at the historical background of the term *science*. The concept *science* underwent a transforming change about five to six centuries ago ~ as *modern* science made its presence felt in our world.

Old Science

For centuries, perhaps millennia, the concept *science* simply meant knowledge. It didn't mean any particular kind of knowledge, but simply the facts about something that were generally accepted as true at the time. One could have a science of anything ~ mathematics, physics, religion, astrology, music, divination, art, prophecy, etc. It didn't matter how the accepted facts were acquired. Facts could be garnered from logical thinking, observation, speculation, sacred texts, divination, prophecies, astrology, folklore ~ you name it. The science of anything, in the old days, was simply what was accepted as true by most people, regardless of how the knowledge was obtained.

That all changed about half a millennium ago, as the concept *science* morphed into the concept *modern science*. The change was subtle, but extremely profound.

New Science

Modern science is not at all concerned with the facts of a particular matter. Instead, it is concerned with *how* the facts are obtained. Only facts obtained in a particular way can be accepted as true; any other facts obtained in unapproved ways are dismissed by modern science as scientifically unproven ~ and simply idle speculation.

Historic science was concerned with collecting together whatever facts were held as true by society, regardless of how the facts were obtained. Ergo, in the old days science meant "a body of knowledge." Today, modern science is not about a collected body of knowledge but about "process" ~ the process followed to obtain the so-called facts. If the information obtained is not the result of following the process dictated by the grounding assumptions of modern science, then that information is dismissed by modern scientists as unworthy ~ and best ignored by those who consider themselves educated.

Grounding Assumptions

The grounding assumptions that we are going to examine are the grounding assumptions of modern science ~ not historic science.

The first grounding assumption is an assumption in the purest of all the philosophies ~ the philosophy of reality ~ or existence ~ or the state of being.

Modern science embraces ~ without question ~ the assumption that reality is an actuality that is concrete, objective and tangible ~ and knowingly shared by all living, rational persons. Reality is a physical universe delimited by space and time. Reality is something in and of itself, and we find ourselves existing and living and thinking within that reality ~ our physical universe delimited by space and time. This grounding assumption is thought of as *realism*. Realism is the opposite of *idealism*, which embraces a diametrically different grounding assumption.

Let's look at an illustration having to do with the nature of consciousness per se. Consciousness ~ is it cause or effect?

Realism argues that consciousness arises from the physical universe. First, the physical universe. Then, biological life. Then, a human brain. Then individual, human consciousness springing from the physical human brain. Realism holds that consciousness is a product ~ or effect ~ of a biological brain which in turn is a part of a physical universe and dependent upon that physical universe for its very existence.

To the direct contrary, idealism argues that consciousness is the beginning of existential reality, and that consciousness precedes everything else, and produces ~ or causes ~ all that we are aware of. Ergo, idealism holds that the physical universe is the product ~ or effect ~ of consciousness. First

Expressions of Consciousness
2nd book of the *Bubbles of Consciousness* book series

consciousness, then the physical universe and everything that is in it, including living human beings.

It's easy to see how realism and idealism directly oppose each other regarding the first grounding assumption. Modern science ~ without question ~ embraces realism and rejects idealism.

The second grounding assumption that modern science accepts without question is that across the physical universe the dynamics and laws of nature are constant.

An example. If gravity pulls two objects together in one part of our physical universe, it will pull objects together in a similar way under similar circumstances in any other part of our physical universe. Another example. If electricity will generate a magnetic field in a coil of metal wire, it will do exactly the same thing in any other part of our physical universe under similar circumstances. Again, the second assumption is that the laws of nature are constant across our entire physical universe.

The third grounding assumption of modern science is that these constant laws of nature can be ascertained ~ or determined ~ thru orderly observation and disciplined experimentation.

Sacred Goal

This fact-finding process of orderly observation and disciplined experimentation is often thought of as empiricism. Modern science's fact-finding process of systematic observation and experimentation must be experienced by the modern scientist thru the five senses of hearing, seeing, smelling, tasting, or touching, or a combination thereof. In other words, the process must be experienced physically.

In brief, the modern-day scientist will conduct a series of observations, possibly detect a law of nature, and then use scientifically exacting experimentation to determine if a law of nature has actually been discovered thru the preceding observations. If successful, the modern scientist will then declare that he or she has made a bone fide scientific discovery that should hold true anywhere and everywhere in the universe, in accordance with the first and second grounding assumptions.

What would be the sacred goal of a philosophy-of-life such as modern science? It would be tempting to say that the sacred goal is to improve the lot of humanity, but that's probably simplistic. The sacred goal of modern science is simply power ~ more particularly, the power to reshape, or refashion, one's existential condition to suit oneself. Let's look at a popular example.

Once humanity discovered the natural laws of nuclear fission, different groups of humans used that newly found knowledge to alter their existential conditions in different ways. One group of humans used that newly found knowledge to bring a quick end to a brutal global war (atomic bombs dropped on an enemy's major population centers). Another group of humans used that newly found knowledge to generate more electrical power for the masses (nuclear power generating stations). In either case humans were using the newly found knowledge to alter their existential condition to an alteration that was more savory. That's the sacred goal of modern science ~ to find and use laws of nature to bring about situational changes determined to be beneficial depending upon whatever human agenda is in play.

Path to the Sacred Goal

Exactly how do modern scientists go about practicing modern science? How is the practice of modern science kept within the confines of the three grounding assumptions? Without tight discipline, modern science could easily devolve back into historic science ~ a collection of accepted facts without much concern as to where the facts came from.

We already know that scientific observations must be gathered empirically ~ that is ~ witnessed by one or more of the five human physical senses of hearing, seeing, smelling, tasting, or touching. Mental insight and intuition are ruled out. Remember modern science's platitude ~ "can it be caught in a test tube?" The first grounding assumption demands empiricism.

We also know that disciplined experimentation is needed to assure us that our empirical observations have led us to the discovery of one of the laws of nature. Predications and hypotheses must be generated that can be proven either true or false. Experiments must be designed with tight controls so that confounding variables and false explanations can be ruled out. It is the third grounding assumption that calls for disciplined experimentation. In its essence, experimentation is a strategy to tighten and control empirical observations to the degree that we can attempt to determine a heretofore hidden law of nature with certainty.

However, it is the second grounding assumption that leads us to the hard-nosed core of modern scientific practice. The second grounding assumption assumes the constancy of nature ~ that the laws of nature are constant across physical reality. If the laws of nature are indeed constant, then it is reasonable to expect that bona fide experimental results can be duplicated anywhere in the physical universe.

And that is the key requirement of the second grounding assumption of modern science ~ *replication*. No matter how carefully the observations are carried out, and no matter how carefully the experimentation is conducted ~ if the findings cannot be replicated elsewhere by other scientists, then new scientific fact has not been established. The first and third grounding assumptions may have been met, but not the second one.

And that indeed is how the practice of modern science is celebrated. If a modern-day scientist comes up with new scientific results that can be replicated by other scientists in other locations, then everyone cheers for the findings. If not, then the work continues to produce replicable results. All three grounding assumptions must be observed and honored in the practice of modern science. All three ~ no exceptions.

Some Scientific Contributions

Let's briefly review the contributions of some of the better known pioneering modern scientists.

Nicolaus Copernicus (1473-1543) was an astronomer and mathematician who lived in the Polish-Germanic region of northern Europe. Copernicus formulated the scientific theory that the planets revolved around the sun. At that time, catholic humanity believed that the planets and the sun revolved around the earth. Copernicus' book entitled *On the Revolutions of the Celestial Spheres* caused quite a stir ~ of course ~ and is considered one of the major founding contributions to modern scientific theory.

Francis Bacon (1561-1626) was a prominent political leader and thinker in England during the English Renaissance. He is considered a founding father of modern science's demand for disciplined, empirical observation when conducting scientific research, especially controlled experimentation. His dictum for scientific inquiry is still largely followed today. Bacon strongly endorsed realism and rejected idealism. He declared that the proper purpose of modern scientific inquiry is to uncover the hidden laws of nature so that these laws could be used to develop new inventions that would improve humanity's lot on earth.

Galileo Galilei (1564-1642) was an Italian scientist who is best remembered for his contributions to modern astronomy. His observations supported Copernicus' theory of heliocentrism, and caused him to incur the wrath of the Roman Catholic Church ~ which dogmatically still held that the sun and planets revolved around the earth. The Roman Inquisition formally found Galileo guilty of heresy against the Church, and forced him to publicly recant to avoid the severe punishments reserved for heretics. Galileo was kept under house rest for the rest of his life.

Rene Descartes (1596-1650) was a French thinker who is considered a founder of modern philosophy. He is probably best known for his contributions to mathematics ~ the Cartesian coordinate system and analytic geometry ~ both precursors to mathematical calculus. Descartes is the Renaissance philosopher known for his assertion that "I think, therefore I am." (Note the quiet argument for idealism.)

Isaac Newton (1642-1727) was an English scientist and a major founder of the scientific revolution during the European Renaissance. His laws of gravitation, and how gravitation affects the movement of bodies in space, further supported Copernicus' theory of heliocentrism. His book entitled *Philosophiae Naturalis Principia Mathematica* is considered a foundational text in non-quantum mechanics.

Gottfried Leibniz (1646-1716) was a German philosopher and mathematician. Leibniz is probably best remembered for his development of mathematical calculus as we apply it today. He also made major contributions to the early development of mechanical calculators, together with contributions to the practical use of the binary numbering system ~ a series of 1's and 0's ~ still the basis of computation in today's ubiquitous computers.

Benjamin Franklin (1706-1790) was an extremely well known American during the founding days of the United States. Franklin was one of the early theorists and experimenters with lightning and electricity. Franklin was a prolific inventor, with the Franklin stove, bifocal glasses and lightning rod being some of his more popular creations. Franklin was also an early proponent of the wave theory of light ~ a precursor to today's popular quantum theories.

Charles Darwin (1809-1882) was an Englishman renowned for his theories concerning the development and progression of biological life on earth. His most controversial holding was that ~ over long stretches of time ~ the struggle for survival in nature caused the best members of a species to survive, resulting in what he termed "evolution" thru the "natural selection of the fittest.". His famous book entitled *On the*

Origin of Species used this argument to attempt to explain the wide-ranging diversity found in biological life. His theories are still controversial today, especially with orthodox religious populations.

Louis Pasteur (1822-1895) was a French chemist famous for his work in the micro-biological areas. He invented vaccination and pasteurization, still used globally today to control pathogenic outbreaks. His reputation as the founding father of microbiology is probably well deserved. His inventions allowed humanity to control and contain many age-old diseases and plagues.

Thomas Edison (1847-1931) was an American scientific inventor who had a big hand in bringing about our modern world. Edison had more than 1,000 US patents covering his many inventions. Inventions he is famous for are the incandescent light bulb, record player and movie camera. Other Edison inventions contributed to the development of light and power utilities and the telecommunications industries.

Alexander Bell (1847-1922) was a scientific inventor known for his invention of the telephone. His professional career spanned Scotland, England, and the United States. His invention was foundational to the rise of the telecommunications industries.

Marie Curie (1867-1934) was a Polish-French scientist known for her innovative research in the field of radioactivity. Her numerous pioneering accomplishments caused her to become the first woman to achieve first place standing in a number of competitive, professional arenas. Nuclear and radiological applications in today's medical health industries can be traced back to Curie's breakthrough scientific research.

Albert Einstein (1879-1955) is best known for his theory of general relativity, and his influence in the field of quantum mechanics. Born in Germany, Einstein finished his professional career in the United States. Einstein was instrumental in warning political leaders of the horrors that could arise from the weaponization of nuclear research.

These are some of the better known pioneering modern scientists and their more notable contributions in the emergence of modern science.

Stance Toward Earthly Utopia

Let's turn now to our other research questions and examine how modern science addresses those concerns. We'll start with modern science's stance toward the self.

Nothing and no one is exempt from the scrutinizing glare of modern science's tightly focused methodology ~ as long as it can be "caught empirically." That also goes for the human "self" ~ it also is considered fair game as an object of study. Modern science generally handles this focus on the human self through the scientific discipline known as *psychology*. Psychology attempts to understand the dynamics of the human self, including both thought and behavior. One of the founding scientists in the analysis of the human self ~ psychoanalysis ~was the Austrian medical doctor Sigmund Freud (1856-1939) who is world-famous for his seminal work entitled *The Interpretation of Dreams*.

Others are also considered fair game for the scrutinizing glare of modern science. Scientific disciplines such as sociology, politics, international relations, economics, anthropology ~ to name just a few ~ study the interactions of singular human individuals amongst themselves. Again, research must be empirical and conform to all the grounding assumptions of modern science.

The boundary between self and other is physical ~ to be sure ~ and unbreachable. Remember, the first grounding assumption assumes reality to be a physical actuality. As long as individual selves are singularly encapsulated within separate human bodies, self and other can never truly commingle or become each other. However, they do share a commonality ~ they are both considered acceptable objects of study in the practice of modern science.

What about the stance that modern science has toward achieving a utopia here on earth? Modern science too wants to achieve an earthly utopia ~ by using the laws of nature to bring about new technology to solve human problems. Modern science has indeed done that, but the side effects are proving toxic.

Perchance the blinders that modern science has imposed upon itself ~ empiricism only ~ contribute to this issue of modern science's poisonous side effects.

In any case, we will have to be cautious in using modern science in our quest for a quick, earthly utopia. We want the blessings without the cursings ~ the wondrous technology without the poisonous side effects. Since modern science is a very predominant conventional thinking of the day all around our planet, we will have to deal with it one way or the other.

Chapter 14 - Summarizing the Analysis

Now that we have submitted our eleven major expressions of human conventional thinking to a common analytic grid, we need to conveniently summarize our findings, particularly with regards to our seventh research question ~ *what is each philosophy-of-life's stance toward quickly achieving a relative utopia here and now on this our earthly home?* Our other six research questions helped us to understand what each particular expression of conventional thinking was all about. However, it is the seventh research question that keeps us in focus as to the overall purpose of this *Bubbles of Consciousness* book series on collective human consciousness ~ we want to somehow quickly revitalize our planetary home so that it can continue to sustain human life as we would like to enjoy it. This is ~ so to speak ~ our work-table project.

Our sample of major expressions of conventional thinking for analytic understanding, again in alphabetical order, is:

Buddhism

Capitalism

Christianity

Communism

Confucianism

Daoism

Hinduism

Individualism

Islam

Judaism

Science

We will try to be succinct in our distillation so that we can hopefully arrive as close as possible to an at-a-glance summarization.

Buddhism is a philosophy-of-life that strictly advocates escape from the earthly human condition. Improving the earthly condition in any way is not at all within its purview. It does promote an admirable level of social ethics and morality, but not to improve the human condition ~ rather to hasten a permanent earthly escape for the presumedly suffering individual. Its emphasis on compassionate values might be useful, but other philosophies-of-life also promote compassionate values. In view of these findings, Buddhism can reasonably be discarded from our work-table.

Capitalism cannot be safely removed from our work-table. It is today's most popular economic model, and whether we like it or not, it will have to be dealt with. Capitalism is an unbeatable producer of highly sought-after mass consumer goods, but it's also an underhanded architect of class-stratified societies. Due to both its advantages and disadvantages, we'll have to be careful in how we handle capitalism as we try to arrive at a path to joyful environmental renewal without incurring negative social consequences.

Christianity is the largest organized religion today, in terms of professing adherents. Its message is one of love, sacrifice, and a promised utopia on earth. It has been waiting for about 2,000 years for its promised utopia. Unfortunately, given the pressing environmental crisis that humanity faces today, waiting is no longer an option. Given its optimistic stance toward the possibility of an earthly utopia, we'll keep it on our work-table for the moment. However, we'll bear in mind that its other-worldly patience in waiting for an earthly utopia can be detrimental to our own interest in a much quicker ~ and hopefully a more immediate ~ solution.

Communism has the admirable goal of the quick establishment of a social utopia here on earth. Its proposed utopia has plenty for all, and has no class stratification capable of generating inner-societal envies and hostilities. It's a wonderful vision for all of humanity. However, communism mandates the use of mass violence to bring about this utopian vision. Due to its advocacy of violence in bringing about an earthly utopia, we will remove it from our work-table. The earthly utopia we seek ~ we do not want it stained with blood. That would be a bad foundation to build on.

Confucianism also wants to establish a social utopia here on earth. It proposes to do this by educating individuals into proper thinking and behavior. However, given that overall human intelligence is being increasingly eroded by pervasive drug abuse, the teachability of human beings may be in decline, together with the historic ability of humans to adapt to changing circumstances. Given its stance on earthly utopias, we definitely want to keep Confucianism on our work-bench, but we will also need to keep an eye on the progression ~ or retrogression ~ of human intelligence, and how that will affect humanity's ability to adapt its thinking and behavior in a timely fashion to our quickly-changing environmental conditions.

Daoism offers an immediate earthly utopia to anyone ~ any individual ~ who is in complete harmony with the natural flow of things. Its promise is aimed at the individual, and not necessarily aimed at the collective. Still, this has promise for our own goal. Its recommended ethics of goodwill, simplicity and modesty may also be of promise to us. We definitely want to keep Daoism on our work-table. Even though its promise of utopia is aimed at the individual, it may have social applications for us today. It is interesting to note that Daoism's utopian requirement to be in harmony with the natural flow of things brings to mind how our scientific revolutions seem to have gotten us a lot of "push-back" from nature.

Hinduism does not embrace the concept of an earthly paradise. It too advocates permanent escape from earthly existence. However, the high value it places on tolerance could be of use to us in our own formulation for a new environmental and social utopia. Its acceptance of reincarnation is also in harmony with our earlier research. Due to this, we will keep it on our work-bench, remembering to bear in mind that even though Hinduism does not support the concept of an earthly utopia, it may still be of utility to our project.

Individualism is a condition of collective human consciousness that we will have to deal with whether we like it or not. The singularity of human physiology drives human individuality. And ~ it is individuals who make up human society. We'll need to keep individuality on our work-table to make sure that we don't overlook the fact that our proposed new utopia will be made up of singular human beings ~ and that the wide-ranging needs of all these multitudinous individuals will have to be addressed and met if our proposed utopia is to have a chance.

Islamism is the world's second largest organized religion today, and growing. It doesn't hold out the hope of an earthly utopia, but rather a utopia for some after death. Earthly existence is viewed more as a proving or testing ground for permanent assignment in an afterlife. This stance, of course, is not of much use to anyone trying to bring about a utopia here and now. However, its message of peace and goodwill and compassionate sharing can be very useful in any utopia, and for that reason alone we will want to keep it on our work-table.

Judaism is a very old religion that has had a tremendous impact on other philosophies-of-life. Its focus is very much on the here-and-now, and it values action far more than lip service. In fact, Judaism would like for every individual presently living to think and act as if they were a utopian citizen right now. That could be challenging, because the Judaic ethical requirements are relatively daunting. However, given its determined focus on utopian behavior in the here-and-now, we will want to keep it on our work-table.

Science has revolutionized the way humans live, providing exciting new possibilities together with daunting consequences. We need to keep it on our work-table because it is the architect and designer of our modern world. In bringing about our new earthly utopia, we very much want to keep the goodies that science has given to us, but we don't wish to continue with the awful side effects. That's a very fine line to tiptoe around, and we will have to be extremely cautious in incorporating science into our new vision.

So ~ let's see where this has left us. We have summarized the findings regarding our chosen eleven major expressions of conventional thinking, and they differ on their helpfulness toward our utopia project.

Two expressions have been dismissed from our further consideration for lack of distinct meaningful utility ~ Buddhism and Communism.

Six expressions are being kept for our further consideration because they may have something positive or useful to offer to our proposed, new utopia ~ Christianity, Confucianism, Daoism, Hinduism, Islam and Judaism.

Three expressions are being kept for our further consideration because they simply cannot be ignored ~ Capitalism, Individualism and Science ~ and also may have something positive or useful to offer to our proposed, new utopia.

We will return to this in a subsequent book. In the meantime, let's move forward to the issue of "exactly who owns conventional thinking?"

Chapter 15 – The Question of Ownership

We have talked about conventional thinking in an earlier book (*The Edges of Consciousness*), and in an earlier chapter of this book (*Chapter 1 - Set Up ~ What We Propose to Do*). What we'll do in this chapter (*Chapter 15 - The Question of Owner-ship*) is bring together what we have discussed so far, and more thoroughly discuss the question of ~ who owns, or is responsi-ble for, or controls ~ conventional thinking.

Before we get into the ownership question, we'll first re-view exactly what conventional thinking is, and why conven-tional thinking is so important to our quest for a fast, relative utopia.

Nature of Conventional Thinking

Conventional thinking is an expression of collective hu-man consciousness. The key word here is *collective*. We're not talking about the consciousness of one individual, but the *col-lective* consciousness of a large group of individuals ~ the *shared* consciousness of all these individuals, to be exact. What is shared are ideas, feelings, expectations, ways of thinking and doing things, etc. ~ and even more fundamentally ~ how existential reality is conceptualized. Conventional thinking is a form of group-think ~ not necessarily at the micro level ~ but rather more at the meso or macro levels. Let's look at some examples.

Everyone has heard the term *corporate culture*. Corporate culture is an excellent example of conventional thinking ~ or collective human consciousness ~ at the meso level. The corporate personnel of any company tend to think and act the same way ~ to the same beat of the same corporate drum. Those who don't think and act in lockstep with the group ~ in this case the other employees of the company ~ find that over time they don't fit in and then find themselves on the outside looking in, either through resignations or firings. It's either "get with the team or get lost." This meso group-think in the corporate world is so manifestly typical of corporate behavioral dynamics that it can be considered ubiquitous. This is an instance of conventional thinking at the meso level in the corporate world. Ditto for all organizations ~ whether private or public ~ or whether for-profit or not-for-profit. Conventional thinking at the meso level is the glue that holds the organization together and keeps the group marching in the same direction.

Conventional thinking at the macro levels involves much larger populations of individuals. The sharing is the same. Again, all members of the particular population share the same ideas, feelings, expectations, ways of thinking and doing things, etc. ~ and even more fundamentally ~ how existential reality is conceptualized.

Group-think within nations or religions provides excellent examples of conventional thinking at the macro level. Conventional thinking at the national level is usually thought of as culture. Conventional thinking at the religious level can readily be thought of as philosophies-of-life. It is generally well accepted that all nations have their unique culture, or way of thinking ~ and that religious organizations offer a unique philosophy-of-life, or way of thinking. That's primarily how the nation or religion differentiates itself from other nations or religions ~ through the distinctiveness of their conventional thinking ~ or, the distinctiveness of their particular expression of collective human consciousness.

Now that we have recapped what conventional thinking is, let's look at why conventional thinking is so important in our quest for a fast, relative utopia.

Importance to Utopian Goal

In our earlier book (*The Edges of Consciousness*) we noted that our ESP abilities seem to lie at the edges of our consciousness because rote conventional thinking occupies the massive center of our consciousness ~ thereby pushing our ESP abilities way out to the sides. This situation is crucial because we wish to use our ESP abilities to help us achieve a quick, relative utopia. However, with conventional thinking occupying the center of consciousness, ESP abilities will remain at the edges. We wish to bring ESP abilities from the edges into the center of consciousness, where we can better utilize them in a deliberate, conscious way. But, conventional thinking is blocking. That's why we find ourselves having to deal with this thing called "conventional thinking."

So, the question ~ *"why is conventional thinking so important in our quest for a fast, relative utopia"* ~ morphs into this more exacting question ~ *"why does conventional thinking occupy the center of human consciousness?"*

The root answer probably lies in the innate sociability of human beings. We might be singular individuals, but we are singular individuals that like to have other individuals around us. We need them, and they need us. There is strength in numbers, especially when facing the perils of daily existence, which can easily overwhelm the stray individual. We like to share our lives with others ~ our thoughts, our feelings, our experiences, our hopes and dreams. This mutual sharing is very important to the human being.

Of course, mutual sharing is enhanced when individuals are similar in their make-up, especially in the way they think. The more we think alike, the easier it is to share ~ it becomes almost empathic. It is difficult to share when the other person thinks differently. We're more comfortable when others have similar thinking to our own. We feel more secure, and vastly enjoy it when the thoughts of others mirror and reinforce our own ideas. That makes us feel good. People with similar ideas and feelings are attracted to each other, and therein arises the genesis of conventional thinking.

Since conventional thinking is such a comfort and security to us, it easily becomes central in consciousness. We cling to it. Without conventional thinking allowing us to think and act together as a unity, we would become as strangers passing in the night, singularly at the mercies of the manifold perils of ordinary existence.

Conventional thinking is very resistant to change. We don't want to let go of the personal comfort and sense of security that it provides. Then we'd have to think for ourselves, with the uncertainty that comes with that. "Better to stay in the comfort zone."

And, of course, we automatically teach it ~ or share it ~ with our kids because that's the way we are thinking ourselves. So, conventional thinking rolls on from generation to generation ~ both enhancing our sociability and providing us with the needed feeling of comfort and security. It probably takes both a very determined original thinker and a stroke of rare luck to have any chance at modifying conventional thinking.

So, who owns it? Who is responsible for it? Who controls it? If we are going to deal effectively with conventional thinking, we need answers to these questions.

Collective Ownership

Obviously, the collective owns it. Without a large group of people sharing their conceptualizations of existential reality, there would not be any group-think, or conventional thinking. Collective thinking springs from a population thinking collectively as one ~ ergo, conventional thinking. Consequently, the collective not only "owns" conventional thinking, but also is responsible for it. However, the question of ~ "who controls it?" ~ is a completely different matter.

Controlled Individuals

To the degree that the individual internalizes the conventional thinking that the individual is immersed in ~ to that same degree conventional thinking actually controls the individual. The individual thinks that it is their own thinking, having lost any sense of where their thinking initially came from. Children don't really remember their childhood socialization.

As adults they will say, "Nobody tells me what to think! This is my thinking; I've always thought like this!"

They think that they are in control of their own existence, but actually the conventional thinking around them that they have so thoroughly internalized since birth is directing their thought and behavior ~ and they are totally unaware of that dynamic.

Something to think about. We are so completely comfortable in thinking that we are our own person ~ but really it is a huge population of people mindlessly thinking for us. We've just lost sight of that.

We'll come back to this discussion of conventional think-ings ~ or expressions of collective human consciousness ~ in later books ~ and how to best deal with it.

Postscript

In this book we have looked at conventional thinkings, or different expressions of collective human consciousness. We've questioned to what degree the various conventional thinkings examined can contribute to our quest for a fast, relative utopia. We've explored a bit more thoroughly the nature of conventional thinking, including its genesis and its dynamic effect on human thought, together with its importance to our purpose.

We've also noted that, given the nature of conventional thinking, modifying it in any way can be an arduous undertaking ~ and that any attempt at modification will usually be characterized by a very determined original thinker together with some very good luck.

In our next book we'll chart the flow of human conventional thinking over both time and place. In a certain way, we can expect our next book to actually be a book about successful original thinkers ~ as they appear over time.

~ 'til we meet again ~

We Are

"bubbles of consciousness"

Floating Together

Thru the challenges of Today

And

Into the Promises of Tomorrow

Thanks for visiting

this book series